Special Thanks

This book would not have been possible without the help and assistance of the following traders, analysts and friends:

John Bollinger
Peter Eliades
Curtis Arnold
Stan Ehrlich
Arthur Rabatin
Mister X (you know who you are)
Franz Wanovits
Ed Dobson
Nelson Freeburg
Tim Slater
Charles LeBeau
Perry Kaufman
...and many others

This book is dedicated to my daughter
Gabriela

TRADERS PRESS, INC.®
I N C O R P O R A T E D
PO BOX 6206
GREENVILLE, SC 29606

Books and Gifts
for Investors and Traders

BEGINNERS GUIDE TO COMPUTER ASSISTED TRADING

PART I

About the Author

Peter Alexander was born in 1953 in New York and was raised in the United States and Austria, where he studied economics at the University of Commerce in Vienna. Mr. Alexander has been active in the development of financial software and trading systems since 1991. Among other innovations, he was first to develop a Japanese Candlestick charting program. Mr. Alexander is also active as an Internet consultant, specializing in financial web sites. In this capacity he has been a chairman and speaker at over a dozen international conferences. He currently resides in Boca Raton, Florida.

Introduction

As the title *Beginners Guide to Computer Assisted Trading* implies, this book is intended as a complete guide for the novice trader, from selecting the appropriate markets to trade, choosing the right hard and software, technical analysis basics, to providing tips and tricks from some of the best known professionals in the business. I can remember how difficult it was when I started out trading several years ago to get a hold of and use all the "right" tools I felt I needed. Several books on technical analysis, one on trading futures, one on stocks, *Barron's, The Wall Street Journal,* a PC, software, data, etc. I was literally buried in stuff to read and study. To top it off, I talked to all kinds of investment "professionals," brokers, analysts and bankers, assuming they surely knew what the markets would be doing tomorrow. Boy, was I wrong.

I will let you in on a secret (since *you* paid for this book you are entitled to some valuable information, right?). You really don't need 90% of the stuff I just mentioned! Yes, it's true. It probably boils down to the old KISS principle, keep it simple stupid, but I guess we all have to dig through piles of rock in order to find some specks of gold. This book will help eliminate a good deal of "rock-crushing," and get you started in the right direction.

Some of the top industry experts I interviewed for this book include Peter Eliades, John Bollinger, Curtis Arnold, Stan Ehrlich, Walter Bressert and many others. What we talked about were issues like favorite indicators, the importance of money management, trading strategies and general advice for beginners. There are no dedicated interview chapters in this book, *alá Market Wizards*, rather I have incorporated the insight provided by these experts throughout. What makes this book very different from the other ones on the market is that "I tell it like it is," which means that nothing in life is guaranteed, especially not making a quick fortune trading stocks and commodities. You will learn how to use technical analysis, see examples of situations that worked out as anticipated, but also cases when things did not pan out. Being able to cope with losing trades is in fact one of the most important aspects of becoming a successful trader. Sounds crazy, but it's true.

Yes, there are many seemingly small, but very important, details that one has to be aware of. Things like self control, choosing the right markets to trade, mental attitude, and so forth. Come to think of it, this book should sell for three times the price! Just send me 10% of your profits, you can keep the losses. Just kidding, of course. Which brings us to the standard disclaimer: Trading any investment vehicle, (including stocks, commodities, bonds, options, funds), is inherently risky, with the potential for complete loss of capital, or more. Therefore, no part of this book shall be construed as a recommendation to trade, or not to trade. In fact, your life is at your own risk! Seriously now, do ***NOT*** speculate with any money that you cannot absolutely afford to lose. Things like retirement money, the kid's college fund, the house. You get the point.

Having said all this, let's proceed to enter the fascinating world of computerized trading. Who knows, you just may be the next Jesse Livermore or George Soros!

PART I

The Zen of Trading

Technical and Fundamental Analysis –
Two contrary approaches

As mentioned in the introduction there is a lot more to trading than just having a computer, the right software and megabytes of historical data. Trading is more like a fine art than a science. Even if you happen to be one of the rare naturals there are numerous tricks and techniques one can learn from the pros. In the course of gathering material for this book I have spoken with top traders, system developers and analysts from the United States and Europe. Some trade stocks and funds, others commodities and a few play the foreign exchange game. I have incorporated the insight gained from these interviews into this book. What they all have in common is that fundamentals play little or no part in their trading approach.

What is the difference between a **technical** and a **fundamental** trader? A **fundamental** trader bases his trading strategy on the analysis of fundamental data. The main argument for the fundamental approach is that the markets cannot ignore fundamentals indefinitely and will therefore eventually behave in certain manners. Fundamentalists consider **technical** analysis with its myriad of studies and competing indicators to be a bunch of *mumbo-jumbo*.

A few major economic indicators followed by fundamentalists:

- Gross Domestic Product
- Unemployment Rate
- Employment Cost Index
- Productivity
- Inventories
- Consumer Sentiment
- New Housing Starts
- Money Supply
- Industrial Production

Example

Rising interest rates will eventually lead to a decline in stock prices or rising energy prices will in turn lead to an increase in inflation, which in turn will lead to tightening of interest rates by the Federal Reserve Board (FED). While fundamentalists will be proven right eventually, there are three major problems associated with trading on fundamentals alone.

First, it can take a long time until the market starts doing what they are "supposed" to do. There have been instances when interest rates kept on rising for over a year until a subsequent decline in the stock market.

Note

The reason why high interest rates are bad for the stock market is this: when an investor can achieve a high rate of return without risk by putting money into bonds or money market accounts, the stock market becomes much less attractive.

The second problem with the fundamental approach is that the numbers watched by the market change over time. Sometimes CPI is the most closely followed indicator, then its the Employment Cost Index, and all of a sudden it's the Unemployment Rate. On some days several economic indicators are released simultaneously, often with conflicting implications. Having a degree in economics is almost essential to fully understand the implications and significance of these reports.

Thirdly, and to make matters really confusing, markets sometimes react totally contrary to the same piece of news. I find it amusing to watch *CNBC* or read the *Wall Street Journal* to see how an economist or bank analyst "explains" why the market did this or that in reaction to a news event. Especially good fun are the days where the market is up 100 points in the morning and down 100 in the afternoon! What this proves to me is that the people you see on TV are just as clueless as you are. Nobody knows for sure where the market is going to be a day, a week, or even an hour from now. Yet opportunities abound for making serious money.

Another reason why it is so difficult to trade on economic news events is this: one month a small increase in the Unemployment Rate might be perceived as bullish news for the dollar and bearish the next. It all depends on what the markets are *expecting,* and how much of the *expected* news has already been factored into prices. There is a lot of truth to the old traders saying *"Buy the rumor, sell the fact."* During my interview with long time commodity broker seminar speaker Stan Ehrlich, he formulated this a little differently by stating that one should *"Buy the expectation, sell the realization."* It's just another way of saying the same thing.

Example

You may have witnessed days when a stock reacts extremely bullish because of some positive company news just to reverse sharply later in the day. This happens when a group of traders step in to *fade* (trade against) a move. Who knows, maybe they knew that good news was on its way and simply waited for a high price to unload their holdings. Trading news events is very tricky indeed.

Another example: A market has a strong bullish undertone when some negative economic data (as far as the stock market is concerned) is released. The market seemingly ignores the bad news and charges on to new highs without any negative effects.

Clearly, there are countless forces at work, some of which may be totally unknown to you. Banks employ highly paid analysts who do nothing else than come up with "guestimates" on how this or that economic figure is likely to materialize. Believe me, these people have access to vast amounts of information, and yet, sometimes they are right, sometimes almost on target and sometimes very wrong. On average, I would be inclined to say that the predictions of an average analyst are right only 50% of the time!

But the analysts themselves are not really the ones to blame. They are under a lot of pressure from their employers to constantly come up with reports and predictions, simply because the customers expect them. Imagine General Motors calling Citibank to find out where interest rates are going to be in 6 months and they get an answer like "To tell you the truth, we really don't know." There goes the GM account! What most people fear more than anything else is the unknown. That's why any prediction, no matter how absurd, is better than no prediction.

This is where technical analysis can offer some help. A technical analyst gains insight into future market activity by examining price changes over time, knowing that all factors affecting the markets are reflected by the price itself. Supply, demand, company news, outlook, dividend yield, expectations, the weather, they all get built into the price anyway. I know quite a few traders that purposely never read any financial publications, just so they don't get distracted from their own chart analysis.

Common and Lesser-known Rules to Successful Trading

As a reader of this book you are presumably a novice trader. There are a number of old adages and rules that a beginning trader will encounter over and over:

· Cut your losses short and let your profits run
· The trend is your friend
· Nobody ever went broke by taking profits
· Never add to a losing position
· When in doubt, sit out
· Always take windfall profits

...and many others

Each of these sayings contains a grain of truth, yet one may seem to contradict another. That's because there are no absolute truths when it comes to trading! You are not only shooting at moving targets, but you are also wearing dark sunglasses. Everything changes, yet stays the same. Trading is almost a mystical thing. But before we get into any heavy philosophizing, let's examine the hidden truth behind some of these sayings.

Cutting losses short and letting your profits run is probably the most popular and least implemented advice. Why? Because you will have losing trades. Lots of them. You might even have more losing trades than winners. Yet it is possible to make money trading. Make money even though the losers outnumber the winners? Impossible! Not really.

The simple secret is that the winning trades must generate more profits than the money lost with the losing trades. That's why losses from bad trades must be kept small. Remaining in the game is priority one. And being around to catch those runaway markets is only possible if you still have a trading account. Makes sense, doesn't it.

Yet, many new traders will self-destruct in a short time by doing the exact opposite. We have all been raised to believe that to be wrong is bad. Thus we don't want to be wrong. We don't like to admit to others or ourselves when one of our decisions turns out to be wrong. Rather, we have been raised to "stick it out" when things get tough. That's what a responsible adult is expected to do, not run away from the problem and try your luck elsewhere. Yet this is just what a successful trader must do. If a trade goes against you by an amount determined BEFORE entering a trade you get stopped out. Plain and simple. A stop is always placed at the same time you enter the market. Mental stops are no good. Because once you have a trade going you will lose, to some extent, your objectivity. Where and how stops are placed is covered later in the book.

Letting your profits run seems to be just as difficult. Many traders tend to take small profits, believing that "nobody ever went broke by taking profits." They just don't want to give back any money to the market that they already have "earned." They want to feel good about themselves. They want to be able to show their friends/wife/whoever how smart they are. "Hey, I just made $500 in 2 days." You won't hear about the losing trades from somebody like this. Taking small profits and not getting rid of the losers early is a sure formula for going bust. Many successful traders only have 35-50% winning trades and still wind up making money. But their strategy counts on catching the big moves and sticking with them as long as possible. This is not an easy task, but consistently making money in any field is work, and trading is no different.

There are techniques for staying with a trade as long as possible. These are covered in a later chapter. And no, there is no guarantee that they will work 100% of the time.

The trend is your friend is another old time favorite. And indeed, unless you have a crystal ball telling you tomorrow's events today, it is best that you follow the trend. Following the trend means that if prices are going up you are a buyer, if they are going down you are a seller. Remember, you can make money when markets (stocks & commodities) go down by selling short. Many beginners feel uncomfortable selling short since you are betting on the decline of something. Hey, we are trading to make a profit, money, cash, moolah, Any other motive and you will pay dearly with your hard earned cash winding up in somebody else's pocket.

Discipline, discipline, discipline

Trading, or better, trading correctly, involves a great deal of self-discipline. Being able to get out of losing trades, staying with the winning ones, waiting for the right trade and trusting your own judgement requires a great deal of discipline. Very few people are naturally born traders. Most good traders started out by losing money, but they quickly learned from their mistakes and constantly work on themselves, perfecting their trading techniques. The worst thing that can probably happen to a beginning trader is that he/she starts out with a streak of winners. This trader will naturally be inclined to believe that "this is easy," that they are gifted, talented or simply smarter than everybody else. The likely result is that they will start to overtrade and risk too much. It is just a matter of time until this trader is doomed.

In the beginning you should only be concerned with trading the "right" way. Waiting for a setup, selecting the right markets, placing stops, taking as much profit as possible. Don't let the losers discourage you. If you placed your stops correctly the losses will be small. You might want to make notes as to why you entered a trade in the first place and why you were stopped out. Was it just market noise (more or less random swings, then the stop might have been placed too tight), a simple misjudgment or just plain bad luck. You might even have a string of bad trades, 5, 6 or more. I heard of a well-known trader that actually had 25 losing trades in a row! Now that's what I call nerve wrecking. As disappointing as losing trades are, if you apply the proper money management techniques and make a point of learning from your mistakes, you will be around to catch the big moves, compensating for all the smaller losses and more.

Trading is somehow similar to meditation. You do not achieve enlightenment by forcing anything. Rather, enlightenment is a result, almost a by-product, of having gained control of one's thoughts and emotions by performing breathing and concentration exercises.

To use another comparison, trading is akin to learning how to ride a bike. First you ride a bike with those two extra wheels (whatever they are called), then you have dad hold the bike, and guide you while you pedal. The first few times you ride by yourself you will fall. But eventually you will simply ride the bike. You will simply do it without thinking about all the constant weight shifting, balancing and steering involved. If you get to the point where trading is as automatic as riding a bike, then you *may* reach the point of becoming a consistently successful trader.

Why did I emphasize may? I personally believe that timing has a lot to do with anything that happens in our lives. And even if you did all your homework there is a chance that you will wipe out, that is lose your trading capital. The markets have the potential to do this. It might take thirty losing trades in a row. Don't say that this can't happen to you, because it can. It may be unlikely, but then it is also unlikely that red will come up twenty times in a row at a roulette table, yet this is not as rare as you might think. This is why I need to emphasize once again, that you should only trade with money that you can afford to lose (in the case of futures) or do without for a potentially long amount of time (stocks and funds).

Stocks and funds are not without risk as the industry might want you to believe. Many investors have never experienced a true bear market and think that by employing a simple buy and hold strategy they can weather any storm. Well let me tell you, in this century there have been several occasions where buying around the end of a bull market (and contrary to popular belief, nobody really knows when a move is over) took many years to recover just to break-even. Case in point: the Japanese stock market. Stocks can, and sometimes do, lose 50% or more of their value in just one day. Some of them eventually recover, and some don't. So if you think stocks or funds are a sure bet, think again.

Traits that separate winners from losers

If you read publications like *Stocks & Commodities* and *Futures* you might have read articles by these three well-known "trading coaches": Van Tharp, Ruth Roosevelt and Adrienne Toghraie. They don't help you design a mechanical system or offer specific trading advice. Yet the help they offer is invaluable. What they do is analyze a trader's performance to find out which psychological reasons might be resulting in poor trading performance.

While each individual trader might have very personal reasons for self-destructing, the coaches have identified a common set of traits that most winners and losers share. Without getting into details, as the psychological aspect of trading could fill an entire book, here a few of the major findings:

- ■ Winners apply rigorous money management techniques
- ■ Winners have the patience to wait for low-risk, high probability trades
- ■ Winners are not worried by inevitable small losses
- ■ Winners are used to relying on their own judgement
- ■ Winners don't have the urge to tell everybody about their trading activity

- • Losers always doubt themselves, their system
- • Losers often use trading for excitement, as a form of legal gambling

18

- Losers overtrade
- Losers use no or poor money management techniques. Losers subconsciously believe that they don't deserve to consistently make money trading

While these few examples only scratch the surface of a very complex field, they do illustrate how subtle personality traits can influence trading performance. Further reading on this subject matter is highly advised. Serious traders might want to attend regularly held seminars by these experts.

Avoiding Pitfalls

The Experts, the Gurus and the Dartboard

One of the first things a novice trader has to learn is to trust one's own judgement. It does absolutely no good to rely on the advice of others, even if they claim to be experts. Only you know what your time frame, market expectation and loss tolerance is. Taking advice from a broker, relying on a newsletter, or trading your brother-in-law's tips, just because he works for a bank, is a sure recipe for disaster.

Let me give you an example. When I first started trading currencies I had a friend that worked as chief currency dealer in a major bank's treasury department. Even though I only traded small amounts, maybe $50,000 to $100,000 at a time, I could call him directly to place my orders. Trading FX (foreign exchange) is different than trading currency futures, and will be covered briefly later in the book. What happened to me 7 out of 10 times was that when I called to place an order he would say something like "are you sure you want to buy now, I would wait a little longer if I were you," or "put your stop further away." Did the advice of this "expert" make me money? Not at all! Because of his remarks I stayed out of trades that would have turned out profitable for me, or got me out of a trades with larger losses than I had initially anticipated.

Sure, once in a while he was right, as far as my trading was concerned. The only real help I got from him was keeping me posted about upcoming economic news releases. It's not that the guy was a bad trader, not at all. FX traders on a busy day can make up to 300 trades (over 90% of the billions of dollars traded in FX every day is between banks), which can generate a substantial amount of profit for a bank. The problem was that he simply had a totally different time frame and profit target than me. This fellow would follow a 5 or 10 minute chart, not a daily one like I did, trading $5 to 20 million dollars a shot, taking a few ticks profit with each trade.

As you can see we both had totally different objectives and time frames. Even worse is relying on tips from your broker, friends or family members. Hey, if they are so smart, how come they aren't rich and famous, and living in Monte Carlo? Newsletters are equally dangerous. Although there are a few genuinely talented guys out there, trading their own signals, isn't it curious why somebody with a fantastic system would bother to sell their "secrets" to the public for a few dollars?

I have done some programming jobs for very wealthy traders whose system was generating 100% plus per year, for several years in a row. The reason why I believe it was true is because I never found out who they really were (a middleman would give me instructions on what to do), and I never was told more about the system than I needed to know. For those of you who are dying to know more, all I can say is that the system is based on trend following. Sorry, I don't know any further details.

The absolute pits, as far as I am concerned, are the people offering sure-fire ways to make money trading commodities. "Anybody can do it," "All you need is $1000 to start," and "Make as much as you want, $1000, $5000, $10,000 a month" are some of the outrageous claims made. All you have to do is buy XYZ's (substitute a well-known name here) video/audio course and you will be on your way to making incredible riches! Once you have bought the package you will receive an endless list of offers for further "market secrets," updates and invitations for private seminars where the "real" secrets are revealed. Why so many people aren't able to use common sense I don't know. Would you sell a map to the Holy Graile for $299 if you knew where it was? I strongly suspect that the answer is no. But these guys are very clever. They even have seemingly logical explanations for why they are offering their secrets to just a few worthy disciples.

Common explanations include that they already made millions of dollars and now they want others to be able to get wealthy too. Or that the system is strictly limited to 99 customers. Yeah, sure.

At this point it may be enlightening to mention the old dartboard trading system. Every year the Wall Street Journal asks a panel of experts to select a group of stocks that they think will outperform the market during the coming year. Then they hang up the stock pages of the *WSJ* and simply throw darts at it to select a random group of stocks . The amazing thing is that the dartboard stocks often outperform the ones chosen by the pros! Yes, some years the pros did OK, but not consistently, as one would expect. And even when they did better than the dartboard, they usually underperfomed the major market indexes. A fellow trader told me about a variation of the dartboard approach where a chimpanzee was used to choose stocks. He (or she) actually outperformed the index! Before you rush out to buy up all the monkies in town let me tell you another true story which may be easier (and less messy) to duplicate.

This guy wrote a trading system that would simply enter a market at random. Yes, purely by chance. I think the markets traded were currencies and bonds, but that is not important. The program would enter the market at the opening, going either long or short, whatever the random number generator came up with. The system would use a simple money management technique called a trailing stop. The stop was a dollar amount, I believe it was $1000.

If the market went against the system, a maximum of $1000 was lost. If the market moved in favor of the trade, the trailing stop was adjusted on a daily basis so that no more than $1000 would be given back. Whenever a position was closed, the system would once again enter the market the next day on a random basis. Long or short, whatever happened to come up.

The amazing thing is that this system was able to make money, at least on paper! Not a whole lot, but over a 10-year test period the average annual return was about 7%, after a very liberal amount of $100 for slippage and commission per trade. *Interesting isn't it?* But before you start to trade by flipping a coin, you must realize that any hypothetical system cannot take into account the effects of actual trading. One is just not always filled at the stop price and limit moves can throw off any system. Still, hopefully this example illustrates the importance of proper money management techniques.

Selecting the right broker

Finding a good stock or commodity broker is like finding a good doctor – not an easy task. Anybody watching *CNBC* or reading the *Wall Street Journal* or *Investor's Business Daily* will find an immense amount of brokers peddling their services, all claiming to offer fast order execution, great fills and personal, professional service. Alas, we do not live in a perfect world, so don't expect your broker to be any more perfect than the rest of the galaxy. As a buyer of this book it is clear that you want to reach your own trading decisions, so there is no need to use a high-priced full service brokerage. Once again, if all the experts and analysts working for a brokerage had a crystal ball, how come they are still working for a living?

What you are really looking for is an execution only account with a brokerage offering good service and reasonable fees. Be wary of deep-deep discount brokers as these fellows often don't have the staff and equipment to service accounts when markets get fast. Busy signals or long holds are the result. Keep in mind that when markets get really crazy, you may not be able to get through to your broker at all, so once again, be sure that your stops are in place!

The only way to see if the service offered is any good is by recommendation or by trying it out. Instead of putting all your money into one account, split it up and open two accounts with two separate brokerages. Then see how they compare. After how many rings is the phone answered? Is the broker courteous and friendly? A grumpy broker can be a real turn-off. A good broker will get you the best price possible, filling your orders at, or very close to, the current ask (price at which you buy). Brokerages of lesser quality may have traders with less experience, resulting in frequent bad fills. Even though you may be paying a few dollars less commission you are losing much more through bad executions.

To see how good orders are filled try this simple test. Put the exact same order in with both brokers and see how you are filled (your order is executed). No, you don't have to call them both at the same time to do this. All you have to do is place something called a stop order with both brokers. As soon as your price is hit the orders become market orders, which means that you are filled at whatever the prevailing price might be.

Example

Give each the order to buy, say, *50 ATT at 45 stop, GTC* (good till canceled). When ATT hits 45 your order becomes a market order and you are filled at the prevailing ask (offer) price. Compare the fills. Were both at 45 ˘ or did one fill you at 45 3/8? Try this out several times and if one broker consistently gives you bad fills, it's better to close that account. Testing brokerages this way will cost you twice the commission but may be a very wise investment in the long run.

If you are satisfied with the performance of both, it can be good idea to keep both accounts active just in the event that you have trouble reaching one. In addition, many brokerages offer a variety of perks. Free automated real-time quotes, magazine subscriptions and portfolio tracking via a BBS or the Internet. Double the perks by having two accounts!

Caution

Trading stocks via the Internet has become very popular and is advertised heavily as this book is being written. Caution. I personally tested a major Internet brokerage for a few days during December of 1996. I must admit, I liked the concept of trading via the Internet: free real-time quotes, fast order execution, access to my account 24 hours a day, portfolio tracking, etc.

Reality was slightly different. In just three short (yet exciting) days as an Internet stock trader I experienced the following:

Unable to get to the online order placement page twice for over 10 minutes, although my connection was O.K. and other web pages of the brokerage's site came up fine. Two of four open orders were not displayed on the appropriate page the second day. A call to their live brokers (luckily they had some) at least confirmed that the orders were not lost, but "just" temporarily disappeared for some unknown reason. Trying to reach customer service resulted in being on hold for 20 minutes.

The reasons for these "inconveniences," I was later told, were due to the enormous growth of Internet trading during the last year. The equipment was just being upgraded and new software was being installed. This may have been the case, but these problems could have (or maybe even did) cost a trader a considerable amount of money.

My recommendation is to trade via the Internet only if the brokerage offers live brokers as well, and your time frame does not include day trading.

Selecting the Right Market to Trade

Selecting the appropriate markets to trade is one of the most important decisions a trader faces. The reason for this is that it is imperative that the market needs to fit to a trader's style and personality. Trading the wrong market is like going out with the wrong date. It will cost time, money and result in disappointment.

Here are some very general and personal observations about popular markets. As detailed in a later chapter, liquidity, volatility and trading range are three major market characteristics to consider.

Stocks

Trading stocks is probably the best way 'to get your feet wet.' Stick to blue chip stocks in the beginning. Barring any major economic catastrophes, or an incredible streak of bad luck, the chances of doing serious damage to your trading account are pretty small. As this book is being written, the stock market has been in a beautiful bull phase and many people have made handsome profits, at least on paper. Keep in mind that paper profits only become real profits *when the chips are cashed in!*

Contrary to popular belief, stocks are not necessarily a safe bet. A common story heard is that somebody who bought a thousand dollars worth of IBM in 1930 would be a millionaire by now. There are very few investors that have a time frame of 60 plus years. Buying and holding stocks for long periods of time (years) *can* be a trading strategy that works out profitably. But buy at the wrong time and you may have to wait a considerable amount of time before the stock recovers. Investors who bought at the peak of the Japanese bull market are still waiting to break-even.

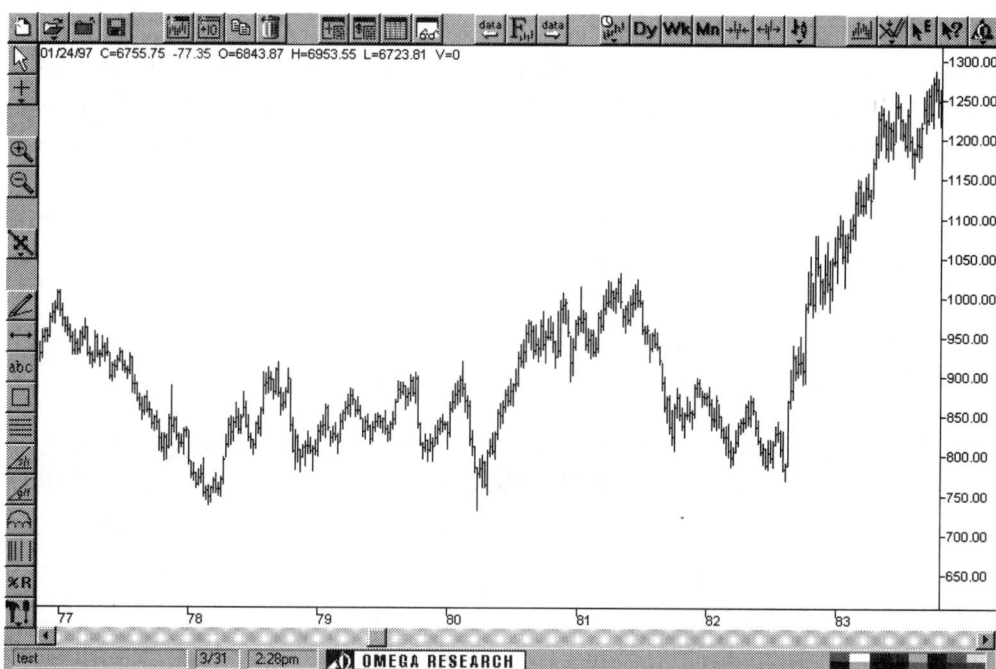

Figure 1. Chart of the Dow Jones Industrial Average 1977-1984. Notice the bear markets starting in 1977 and mid 1981. It took three and a half years for the Dow to get back to the 1000 level after the market turned south after the market peaked around January 1977.

Figure 2. Chart of the Nikkei 225 stock index from January 1992 to June 1994. Buying around the beginning of January 1992 and holding would have meant waiting a year and a half just to get back close to the entry level.

Novices should stick to stocks that are heavily traded. Optionable stocks, these are major stocks with associated options, along with the S&P 500 index stocks are good choices. Be cautious when trading 3rd rate OTC (NASDAQ) stocks. The markets of such stocks are called thin, meaning that the amount of shares traded every day is very small. The result is that the difference between the ask (the price you pay when buying) and the bid (what the broker will pay you when selling) will be larger than with stocks like IBM and GM.

The difference between bid and ask is called the **spread.** The wider the spread, the more difficult it becomes to just reach the break-even point.

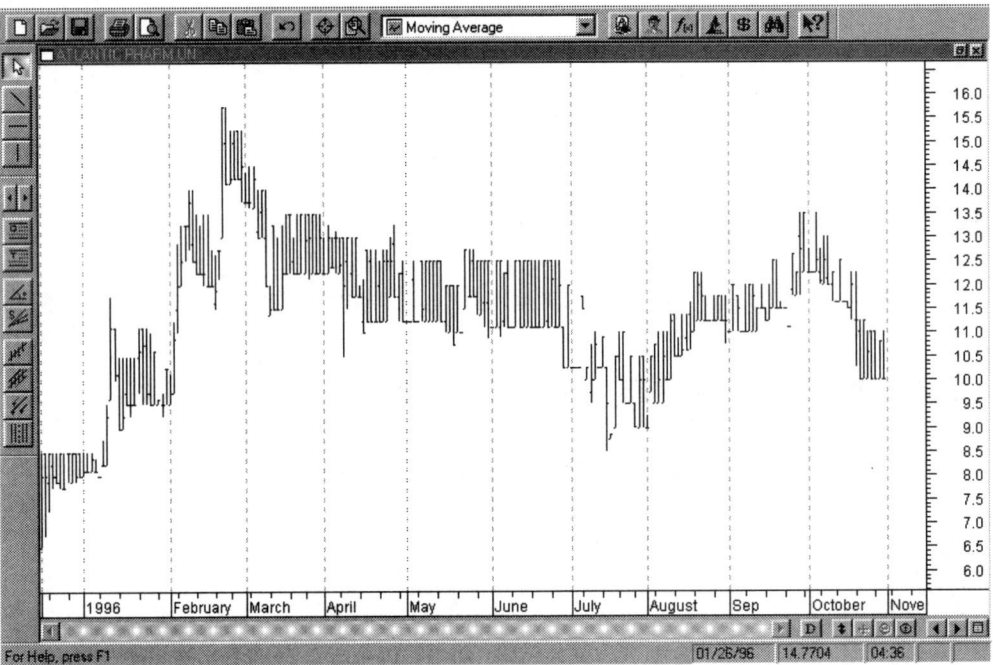

Figure 3. Chart of a stock with small trading volume. Note how the high-low range often remains the same several days in a row.

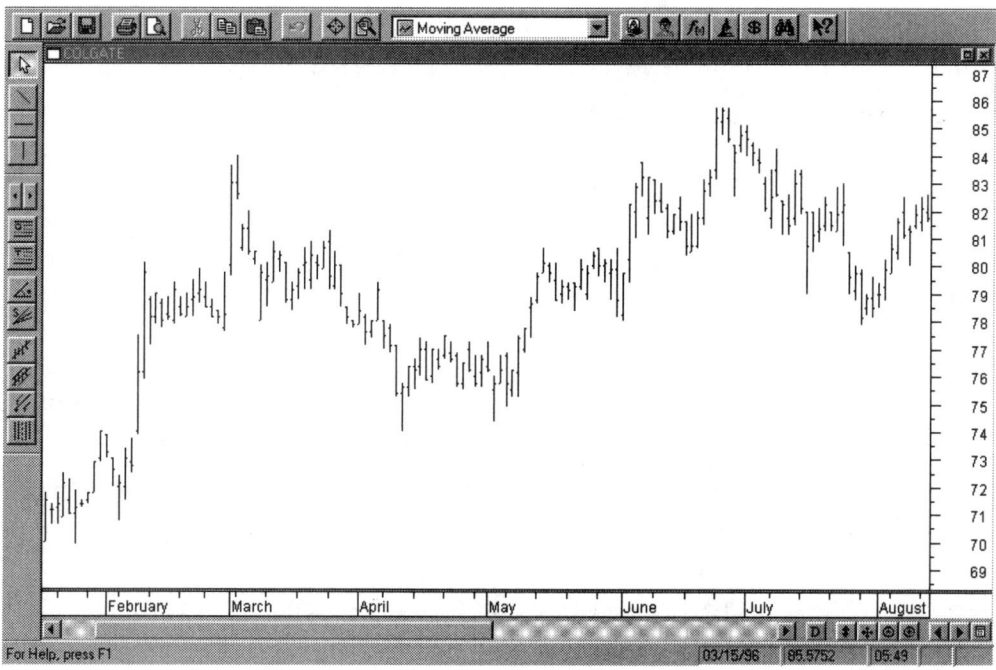

Figure 4. Chart of a stock with high trading volume. Compare the "look" of this chart to the previous one. Technical analysis works best when dealing with very liquid (active) securities.

Opening an account

To open an account a minimum initial deposit of between one and five thousand dollars is required. The two basic types of accounts are *cash* and *margin*. With a cash account you can only keep buying stocks while the account has enough cash to cover the purchase. With a margin account stocks may be financed with borrowed money (by the brokerage). One can borrow up to half the price of a stock against the account's total value.

Example

A trader with $20,000 in a cash account could buy 1000 shares of ABC Corporation at $20. With a margin account, however, the investor can buy 2000 shares of the same stock. As you can imagine, brokerages do not lend money for free. They charge something called a brokers call rate, thus, financing stock purchases in this manner has its costs.

The ability to trade more shares than one could with cash alone adds something called *leverage*. An understanding of leverage is extremely important, especially to commodity traders. Leverage works both ways: If the stock you bought moves in your favor, you make twice the profits. If the stock is sold at a loss, the loss will be twice as much. Margin trading is just like buying something on credit. You can buy a car for just 10% down, but if you crash it the next day the finance company still expects *all* the payments.

Commodities

Trading commodities is for the speculator with ample risk capital. Futures traders must constantly monitor their positions. You cannot buy a commodity and just forget about it. Even markets with low volatility can experience sharp reversals without notice. What makes trading futures so risky and potentially profitable is the amount of leverage involved.

Leverage means that with a small initial *good faith deposit,* called margin, one is able to control a contract of substantial size. A US Treasury Bond future, valued at one million dollars, requires a margin of maybe $3000. The tick size of a T-Bond is measured in 32^{nds}, with each 32nd having a dollar value of $31.25. A one point (32 times $31.25) move has a value of $1000. Daily moves of one or two full points are not uncommon, so you can easily make or lose several thousand dollars in a day. Only you can decide if a market like this is compatible with your trading style and pocketbook.

The margin required is regularly adjusted by your brokerage to reflect market volatility. S&P 500 futures at one time required a margin rate of over $20,000, now it is around $15,000. Every brokerage sets its own margin rate, based on minimums required by the commodity exchanges. The appendix offers a sampling of margin requirements as of April 1997. Opening a commodity trading account usually requires a deposit of at least $5000. Most brokerages pay interest (T-Bill rate) on cash in the account.

A term often heard is the dreaded "margin call." At the end of each trading day your brokerage calculates the value of each position, a process which is called marking to market.

Example

Let's assume you bought a March Eurodollar contract at 95.30 and that the margin rate is $400. Each tick (the smallest amount the price can move) of this market is worth $25. If it closed today at 95.10, you would have a paper loss of $500 per contract. Assuming that there were no additional funds in your trading account besides the initial $400 margin, you could expect a call by your broker the next morning to immediately transfer $100 to bring your margin back up to the required $500. Failure to do so will result in liquidation of the contract by the broker at whatever the current price level may be. Needless to say, traders are 100% liable for any losses incurred.

Getting a margin call is a most unpleasant way of being reminded that the liquidation of a losing trade has been postponed too long.

Spreads

A popular way to trade commodities is something called "spread-trading." Without getting into the intricacies of this trading method (there are books on the market covering techniques in detail), a spread is when a contract month of a given market is bought while another month is sold.

Note

Different contract months have different prices because of various factors, one being something called *carrying charge*. Carrying charges are the costs involved in storing, financing and insuring a commodity. A commodity with a farther out delivery date needs to be stored longer than a nearby one. Various events can influence the difference between these prices, making one contract rise or fall faster than the other, offering trading opportunities. A bull spread is when you buy the month that is rising faster than the other (shorting that one) while a bear spread is when you sell the month declining faster than the other (while buying the other). The actual prices are of no concern to the spread trader. His only concern is the difference between the two.

Spreads can be less volatile than outright positions, since one is long one contract while being short the other and the loss on one will be offset by the gain on the other.

Caution

Markets can behave in a way that it is possible to start losing on both "legs" of a spread.

Spreads can be entered by giving the broker an order to buy a spread or by "legging in," a process that is not recommended. By legging in one first enters one part of the spread (just like entering a plain position) and execute the second leg minutes or hours later. Spreads can be executed "at the market" or by limit orders. Since one is only trading the difference between the value of the two contract months it is usually better to use limit orders.

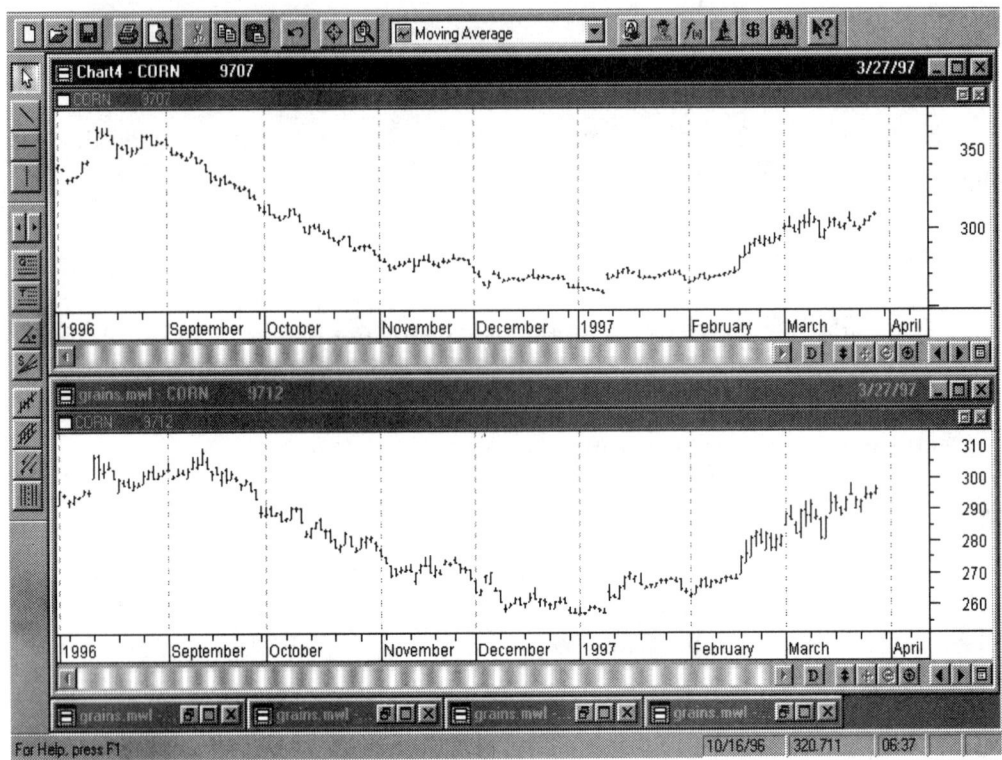

Figure 5. Individual July and December Corn charts.

Figure 6. Spread chart created by subtracting July Corn prices from December Corn prices.

Example

On September 1, 1996 July Corn is at 355 and December Corn is at 304. You expect the July Corn to fall in value faster than the December Corn. The current spread is 51 points and you think it will decrease to 20 or less. Thus you are planning to go short the spread. When shorting you sell high and buy back low. The order you would place with your broker would be something like "this is account 12345, on a spread I want to buy a December Corn Contract, sell a July Corn Contract." Always start with the buy side. In order to keep this example simple let's assume that the order is placed as a market order. In reality it is usually best to use limit orders when dealing with spreads. Four weeks later on October 1, 1996 July Corn is at 311 and December Corn is at 288. As expected, the July contract lost a lot more than the December . The spread is now only 23 points. If the trade were now liquidated, the resulting profit would be 28 points since the spread was sold at 51 points and covered (bought back) at 23 points.

Note

Spread quotes do not necessarily correspond exactly to the individual market quotes. Just because July Corn is trading approximately 50 points higher than March Corn, there may not be any offers in the pit to sell the spread at more than 48 points. It often helps to get a spread quote before placing a spread order.

The main drawback with spreads is that they cost twice the commission (brokers charge a full round-turn when entering a spread and another when exiting), plus the fact that one faces the bid/ask spread twice as well. Twice the bid/ask spread because when entering the spread trade you are buying the ask (with the long leg of the spread) and selling the bid (the short leg of the spread), doing the same in an opposite fashion when closing the position.

Exchanges with good liquidity include currencies traded on the Chicago Mercantile Exchange (CME), CBOT Treasury Bonds and Grains (Corn, Wheat and Soybeans). A relatively tame market I can recommend for novices is the CME Eurodollar. With Eurodollars you can select the amount of volatility by choosing the contract month. The further away the contract month is, the bigger the price movement, but even the nearby month can get "hot" if there are some unexpected interest rate changes.

Mutual Funds

Mutual funds have increased immensely in popularity during the last few years. The notion is that a fund, managed by a professional fund manager, is virtually immune to any serious damage. Sure, a well-managed mutual fund has resources and decision aids available that are out of reach of the average investor.

Most funds, I guess around 98%, are basically bullish funds, betting on rising stock or bond prices. If your economic outlook is somewhat bearish, you might want to talk to your investment advisor about bear funds, or funds which take short positions. Unfortunately, my experience has shown that investment advisor expertise in this area is spotty.

Funds are available with a wide variety of investment objectives. A list of major fund categories follows:

Stocks

- Aggressive Growth
- Small Company
- Index
- Global Equity
- Balanced
- Europe Equity
- Sector
- Precious Metals
- Emerging Markets

Bonds

- High Quality Corporate Bond
- High Yield Corporate Bond (junk bond)
- Municipal Bond (short/intermediate/long-term)
- International Global Bond
- General Government Bond (short/intermediate/long-term)
- Mortgage Backed Government Bond

Be sure to study the prospectus of any fund you plan to invest in to insure that a fund's strategy is compatible with your investment objective. Fund A might always be fully invested in the stock market while fund B could be up to 50% in cash when certain market conditions arise. Another important issue is the fact that a fund's strategy can change over time. A Morningstar (fund rating service) analysis of all mutual funds showed that more than 700 funds had changed their investment strategy over the past two years. Mutual funds are not fail-safe. When bond prices tumble interest rates rise. This spells bad news for bond and stock funds alike. I like to see how a fund I am interested in buying reacts to corrections in the stock market. Funds that show the most resilience are the ones I prefer.

Figure 7. Chart of the S&P 500 going back one year.

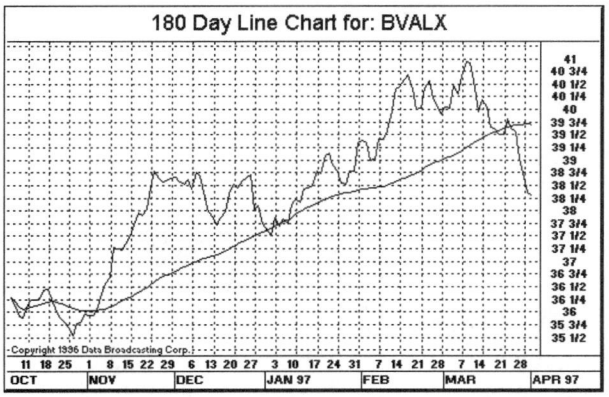

Figure 8. Chart of the Babson Value Fund. The performance of this fund compares favorably to a broad index like the S&P 500.

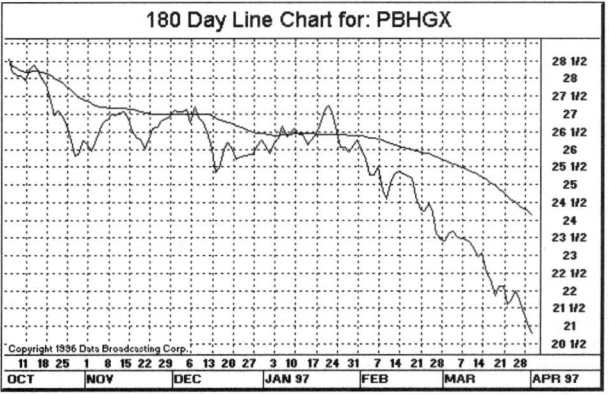

Figure 9. Chart of the PBHG Fund. The performance of this fund does not match that of the S&P and is considerably worse than that of Babson Value.

35

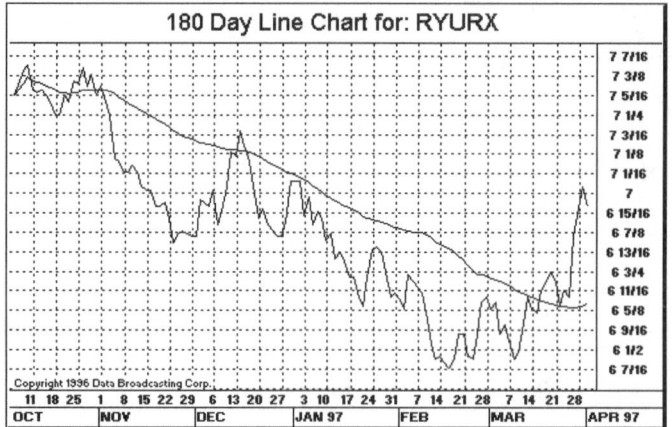

180 Day Line Chart for: RYURX

7 7/16
7 3/8
7 5/16
7 1/4
7 3/16
7 1/8
7 1/16
7
6 15/16
6 7/8
6 13/16
6 3/4
6 11/16
6 5/8
6 9/16
6 1/2
6 7/16

Copyright 1996 Data Broadcasting Corp.

11 18 25 | 1 8 15 22 29 | 6 13 20 27 | 3 10 17 24 31 | 7 14 21 28 | 7 14 21 28
OCT | NOV | DEC | JAN 97 | FEB | MAR | APR 97

Figure 10. Chart of Rydex Ursa, a bear fund. Notice how the fund value increases when the general market turns down. However, this type of fund does not do well in bull markets.

Loaded funds (funds which charge a 3-5 or more percent fee) can take some time before the purchase expense is offset by gains. No-load funds do not charge fees when buying and selling, but note that brokerages may charge a service fee when funds are held less than a minimum amount of time, usually 3-6 months. *Check beforehand.*

According to Peter Eliades, stock market expert, comparing the performance of a stock fund to a broad index like the S&P 500, is a good way to evaluate investment candidates. Sector funds, for example defense funds, are best judged by comparing them with sector indices.

No-load funds cannot be purchased or sold any time during the day like a stock or commodity. Rather, both buying and selling is done at a price called the Net Asset Value (NAV). The NAV is calculated late afternoon New York time. The cutoff time for placing orders to be executed that day is between 2-3 pm. A big minus when trading this type of fund is the fact that the investor has no way of knowing in advance at which price the trade will be filled. The placement of stop and limit orders is also not possible, making no-load funds unsuitable for short-term system trading.

A closed-end fund is a special type of fund which trades just like a stock. It has a bid and ask price and can be bought and sold anytime during the trading day. Close-ends are less popular than regular mutual funds, maybe for the simple reason that brokerages make less commission on them. Just because an investor doesn't have to pay a commission when buying a no-load fund doesn't mean that the brokerage is providing the service because they are doing you a favor. Rather, the fund pays the brokerage a commission for providing customers.

Foreign Exchange (FX)

The probable largest market of all is the *Interbank* foreign exchange market (currency trading between banks). Trillions of dollars change hands every day. FX is traded 24 hours a day, seven days a week. In order to trade currencies directly with a bank's treasury department, or a FX broker, a minimum deposit in the vicinity of $100,000 is required. FX is not recommended for beginners, even when deep pockets (a substantial trading account) are available. Therefore, only the basics will be covered here and the reader is free to gather knowledge by further reading.

The biggest currency markets are between the US Dollar and these currencies: German Mark, British Pound, Swiss Franc, Japanese Yen and Canadian Dollar, followed by the French Franc and Australian Dollar. *Cross rates* are currency pairs that do not directly trade the greenback, like German Mark against the Swiss Franc and British Pound against the Japanese Yen.

Trading size is in so-called 1 Dollar lots (that's 1 million Dollars!), but smaller and larger amounts are common as well. One is not limited by any pre-defined contract size like with exchange traded financial futures. The bid/ask spread in Dollar/Deutschmark when trading a million dollars is around 10 *pips*. A *pip* is the smallest price unit, the same as a tick. The bid/ask spread is narrower, down to 2-3 pips, when trades are in the 5 Dollar vicinity.

Example

You call the Dollar/Mark desk at your bank to get a price for one dollar (one million). The trader quotes 1.6510-20. The quote represents the amount of German Marks a US Dollar can buy, so a dollar is worth 1 Mark and 65.10 Pfennigs. A rising dollar will buy more German Marks, so when you are bullish on the dollar you buy the Dollar by selling Marks to the bank (paying 1.6520 per $). As with any trade, when buying you pay the higher price (1.6520) and receive the lower one (1.6510) when selling.

Caution

Exchange traded Deutschmark futures are quoted the opposite way! Prices are quoted in cents per German Mark. When a trader is bullish on the greenback he sells German Mark contracts short.

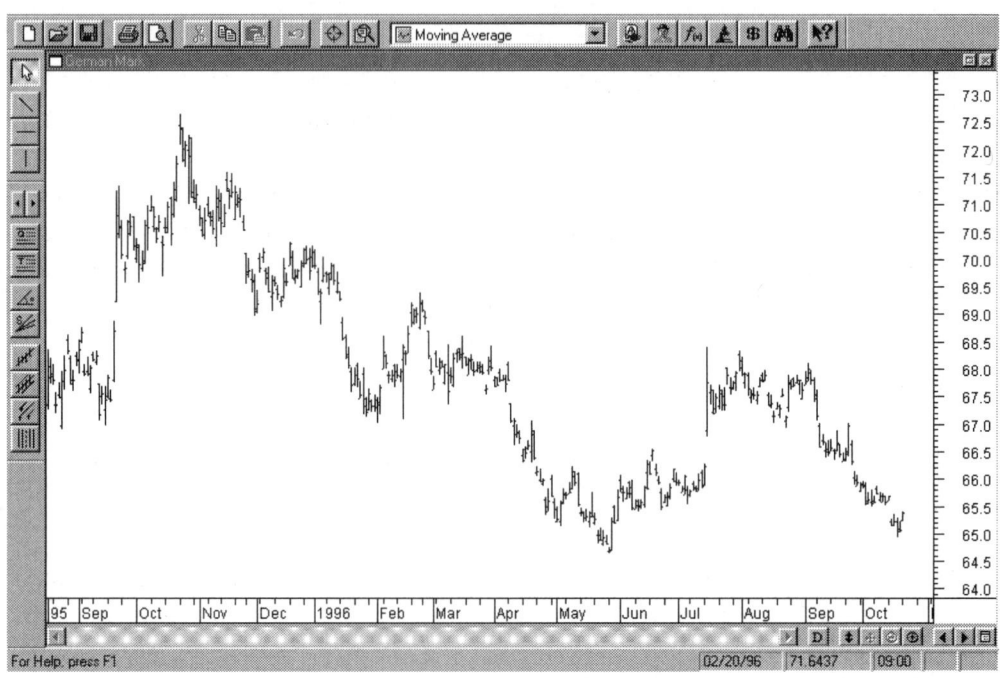

Figure 11. Chart of Deutschmark futures, which are quoted in cents per Deutschmark. Declining prices of this chart mean that the Dollar is rising.

Figure 12. Chart of cash Dollar (Interbank FX) , expressed as Deutschmarks it can buy. Note that the futures chart, when flipped upside down, almost totally resembles the cash Dollar. They do not match exactly, however, since futures only trade for a part of the day.

A big advantage of FX is that trades are filled instantly at a known price. When an FX dealer or broker (sometimes called the *counterparty*) quotes a price and it is accepted, the deal is done. This is one reason why big speculators prefer FX to the regular exchanges. With exchange traded futures it can happen that a trader must wait for some time to find out at which price even a market order was filled! Not knowing at what price a trade was filled can expose a day trader to a considerable amount of risk. How can you get out of a position when you don't even know for certain if, and at what price, a trade was filled!

Options

My opinion regarding options is simple: *stay away from them.* Unless you like gambling and don't mind losing most of the time, stick to the markets discussed previously. I have never met a novice who made money with options by anything else than sheer luck. It is just way too difficult, in my opinion, to not only anticipate a market's direction, but accurately time the move too. Believe me, there is nothing more frustrating and baffling to a beginner than to correctly call a move while the option's price doesn't budge.

The people making money with options are the ones who write (issue) them and that is a game reserved for the big boys with complex analytical software at their disposal.

Order Types

A thorough understanding of order types is essential if unpleasant surprises are to be avoided. Beginners often ask if there is a "best way" to enter and exit a trade, and the answer is unfortunately no. Which order type to use depends on the trading approach, objective and exchange regulations. Certain orders may be acceptable by one exchange and not by another. Some are accepted on a "not-held" basis, which means that execution is not warranted by the exchange! For obvious reasons "not held" orders should be avoided. Check the Appendix for a complete list of order types accepted by major exchanges. As previously mentioned, none of these order types can be used with no-load funds.

Note

Remember, when buying you are paying the *ask* (offer) price. When selling you receive the lower, *bid*, price. The difference between bid and ask is called the *spread*.

Day order

All orders other than a *market order*, which is an order for immediate execution, have a time factor attached to them. A stop or limit order placed as a day order means that it valid only for the current trading day. If the order is not filled that same day, it is discarded.

Good Till Canceled (GTC)

A good till canceled (GTC) order stays in effect until it is either filled or canceled. Traders sometimes forget about their open GTC orders, resulting in big surprises. Brokers constantly get a "Huh? What do you mean I just bought 5 November Soybeans?" when customers are called to report a fill. Traders should check open positions with their brokers on a daily, or at least weekly, basis.

I would suggest every trader close all positions and cancel all open orders before going on vacation. After all, the point of going on vacation is to get away from it all, isn't it? Just imagine if you get a fill while enjoying an African safari (no *CNBC* or *Quotrek* there!). There may be a very unpleasant surprise awaiting you upon your return home.

Note

Certain commodities have day and night trading sessions (GLOBEX). If orders are to be in effect during all sessions this must be specifically requested. Keep in mind that spreads are wider during these less liquid trading periods, which can result in unfavorable fills.

Caution

Stop and limit orders do not provide any protection against gaps. A market can gap (jump higher or lower) during trading hours after an important news event or when a market opens after a holiday or weekend.

Market orders

Buying or selling at the market means that a trader is willing to accept whatever the current bid or ask may be. A market order should be used to enter a trade when you need to get into a market right away. Using any other order type may keep you from getting filled. Day traders who follow a 15-minute, 5-minute or even 1-minute chart usually use market orders to enter and exit trades. Commodity traders must use caution using market orders with certain markets and exchanges, as floor traders will attempt to rip you off with as much as they can get away with.

A variation of a plain market order is the *disregard tape order* (DRT), which gives the floor broker the discretion to delay execution of a market order if he thinks that it might be filled at a better price by doing so. DRT's are only accepted on a "not held" basis, which means there is no guarantee of fill quality.

Market on open – Market on close

Variations of a plain market order are *market on open* and *market on close.* As the names imply, these orders are filled at the market during the opening and closing range. Market on close has been dubbed *murder on close,* since wide price swings are frequent, resulting in bad fills.

Stops

Buy and sell stops are used to enter and exit trades when a specific price level has been hit. When this is the case the order becomes a market order and is filled as such. Stops are either used to limit losses (also called a stop-loss order) or to enter a trade when a specific price level has been hit. Buy stops are placed at or above the current market and sell stops are place at or below the current market.

Note

With most exchanges, prices have to actually trade at your stop price before the stop order becomes a market order. If you have a stop at 65.50 the order will not go into effect just because the security has been quoted at the price. It needs to actually trade at that price first.

A *trailing stop* is a stop that is adjusted regularly, usually on a daily basis. It is placed under the current price when long, or above the current price when short, locking in some profits while keeping the trade going. Trailing stops are a very good way to stay with a trade as long as possible while preserving capital.

Stop Limit

This is a variation of a simple stop. It instructs the broker to fill the order at your price or better, if possible, once the stop is triggered. Stop limits are placed above the market when buying and below when selling.

Stop Close Only (SCO)

This stop order is executed only during a market's closing range. This kind of stop is sometimes used to avoid being stopped out during a trading session but can be disastrous if the market makes a major move against you.

Stop Limit Close Only (SLCO)

This order can only be triggered and executed during the closing range.

Cancel – Straight Cancel

Use a straight cancel order to terminate an open order.

Cancel Replace

Cancels an open order with the intention to replace it with another one.

Example

Disney has been trading between 50 and 54 and your analysis leads you to the conclusion that a considerable rally could be underway if prices hit 55. You call your broker to buy 1000 Disney at 55 on a stop, good till canceled. The moment Disney trades at that price or higher your order becomes a market order. So, even though you had a stop to buy at 55, the actual fill could be at 55˚, 56 or 54˚.

Example

You went long one June Eurodollar at 95.40. The most you are willing to lose on this trade is 10 points, which equals $250. Thus an order is placed to sell one June Eurodollar at 95.30 on a stop, GTC (good till canceled).

Limit Orders

A limit order guarantees that an order will only be filled at your price or better. This is in contrast to stop orders, which do not guarantee a specific price.

Example

A trader bought 500 shares of Exxon at 67˘. Share prices have been rising recently and a test of 80 is in the cards today. The trader wants to take some profits and get at least 80 per share, not less. He calls his broker to sell 500 shares of Xerox with a limit of 80. Another way of placing the same order would be to say "sell 500 shares of Xerox at 80 or higher." If Xerox is only quoted 80 (not traded) and then immediately retreats, there is a chance that the order will not be filled.

Important Issues

There are a number of important issues to consider besides market selection. Factors like commission and slippage can make or break trading systems. Slippage refers to the difference between the price that a trader is counting on and the actual fill.

It is quite easy to program trading systems that generate handsome hypothetical profits when commission and slippage are not considered. But alas, we all have to pay dues for the honor of playing the great trading game. As mentioned in the *Selecting the Right Broker* chapter, paying high commissions and getting bad fills are a good recipe for a quick end to any trading career. Do not simply accept bad fills as something that can't be changed, like the weather. Sure, when markets are moving fast even the best broker cannot perform any miracles, but if your stops are always filled one or more ticks away from your price, or market orders aren't confirmed within 15 minutes at the latest, threaten to take your business elsewhere. Tell the trading desk manager why you are unhappy with their service. A threat to switch brokers will carry more weight with active traders, of course.

The following story illustrates how important it is to keep a tight lid on trading expenses.

Example

In the course gathering material for this book I spoke to an asset management company in Europe with a foreign exchange trading system. The system generates a profit of about 15 percent per year trading German Marks, Swiss Francs, British Pound and Japanese Yen. The manager explained to me that is was imperative for the positive performance of the system that the bid/ask spread they received was no more than 3-4 pips. A spread of 7 or more pips would turn this otherwise profitable system into a loser.

Minimum price fluctuation

The minimum price fluctuation is the smallest dollar amount a stock or commodity can change by. With OTC stocks (NASDAQ) this is 1/64 of a dollar, AMEX and NYSE stocks trade in 1/8ths. Things get considerably more complicated with commodities, where the value of the smallest move can range from $1 to $31.25. The appendix offers a complete listing of US commodity markets with their respective contract sizes and minimum price fluctuations.

Commissions

Commissions charged by commodity brokers are based on a "round-turn," sale and purchase. Discount futures brokerages might advertise a round-turn rate of $25-35, while a full-service brokerage often charges $50 and more. Occasionally brokerages offer "teaser rates" of $15 or less for the first few traders or the first month's traders. The difference between a discount and full-service broker is that the discount broker only acts as an order taker. No advice or handholding is given or expected.

With stocks you have to bite the commission bullet twice, once when buying and again when selling. The lowest stock commission rates are now in the $15 vicinity, usually only available when trading via the Internet. Some of the better known Internet brokerages include *Lombard, Etrade* and *E-Schwab*. Of course, do not expect any advice or tips (or even a live broker for that matter) when trading at these discounted rates.

A full-service broker may have a special trading desk for beginners offering assistance and information that can be very helpful. They can answer question like point values, trading hours, recent news affecting the markets and the like. You should not ask them, or expect them to offer, specific trading recommendations. Even though these fellows sit in front of a quote machine day in day out, they do not know where anything will be 3 days from now. If they did, they wouldn't be spending their time on the phone with a bunch of nervous clients, would they?

Liquidity

Liquidity is a term used to describe the amount of "business" going on in a given market. A stock which is a component of the Dow Jones Industrial Average, Caterpillar, for example, is traded constantly, with hundreds of thousands of shares changing hands every day. A lesser known stock traded on NASDAQ might only have a trade volume of a few thousand, or might not even be traded every day. Unless you are a really, really, big trader you will never have any trouble buying or selling Caterpillar, but you could face some trouble with a very small stock.

Why is liquidity such an issue? Because liquidity has a direct effect on prices. Remember, with every financial instrument there is a bid and ask (or offer) quote. Bid is the price that a broker is willing to pay you when you are a seller; ask is the price you have to pay to buy. For example, Microsoft might be quoted at 110 °-110 ∫. A buyer of Microsoft has to pay 110 ∫ per share, a seller will only get 110 °. The difference between the two is called the "spread," which in essence is how brokers make their money. Depending on market conditions and liquidity of the stock, the spread can be very small, maybe an eighth, or wider, ∫ or so. The same principle applies to futures. One of the most liquid commodity markets is the US Treasury Bond. Here the difference between bid and ask is generally only one tick. A tick is the smallest unit by which prices change.

The reason why liquidity is so important should be apparent by now. If you buy a stock where the spread is ∫, prices have to rise 75 cents before you only reach the break-even point (in addition to commissions and transaction fees).

Volatility

Volatility describes how much and how fast prices tend to move up and down. Just like gunpowder is less dangerous to handle than nitroglycerine, some markets have the tendency to behave much more erratic than others. Volatility is not static, it can change very quickly. Wheat may have been trading in a very narrow range for months, but this does not mean this condition will last forever. In fact, long periods of calm are usually followed by explosive moves (called *break-outs*), offering interesting trading opportunities.

Some traders like to stay away from volatile markets. There is nothing inherently bad about an active, volatile market. After all, you can't make money in a market that is going nowhere! You just have to be aware of the risks involved. If you go on a hike through the jungle with the right equipment, you will have a great time, otherwise you may not even survive the first hour. Still, I would recommend that any novice trader start out by choosing markets that are not prone to wide swings. In the beginning the most important thing is to gain confidence and experience, and there is nothing more devastating to a trader's confidence than when he or she is blown out of the market hours or minutes after entering a trade. How can you gauge a market's volatility? By looking at the chart, of course! If wild swings and gaps are rare, you have a candidate. There are even a few indicators that aid in measuring volatility, such as *Chaikin's Volatility Indicator.*

Nothing adds more volatility to markets than unexpected news events. In fact, trying to trade news events is one of the most difficult forms of trading, even if you have a real-time system and a good broker.

Example

A wealthy trader was bearish on the S&P 500 and was looking to short that market. (Selling short is when you sell stocks or commodities, hoping that they will go down in value so you can buy them back later at a lower price, thus realizing a profit). That morning an interview was scheduled on TV that was going to have an effect on the S&P, an economic indicator of some kind, so the trader prepared himself (at least so he thought), by having his broker on the line while watching the live interview on TV.

The moment the person delivering the economic news started speaking with the words "Unfortunately…" the trader gave his broker the order to sell several contracts at the market. Maybe 10 seconds later the trader received his fills, which happened to be limit down (certain commodities can only move up or down a specified amount per day), with the S&P then immediately reversing and closing higher on the day! Needless to say, this trade turned out to be a considerable loser.

This example illustrates the following:

· Always expect the unexpected. The small detail the trader had overlooked was the fact that TV in the United States, even live broadcasts, are on a 7 second delay. Seven seconds can be an eternity when markets are fast.

· Try to avoid placing trades just before or after a major piece of economic data is released (any decent broker can provide you with a calendar of economic release dates). Markets tend to be extremely volatile at these times, so it is often best to wait until 5-30 minutes have passed before entering a trade. Sure, it will happen on occasion that you would have made a killing had you only bought/sold a minute before the announcement. But then you are simply betting, and if that's what you want to do it is better to go back to the bookstore and exchange this book for *A Beginners Guide to Shooting Craps.*

· Don't rely on radio or TV when trading news events. For professional traders it is imperative to have dedicated news feeds, which are not delayed, like the ones provided by Dow Jones or Reuters.

Markets & exchanges to avoid

Besides taking a security's volatility and liquidity into consideration, the exchanges themselves have certain characteristics. For example, commodities traded in New York can be very tricky. Stay away from them. These are markets for people who really know what they are doing. I have several friends who tried trading with market orders there and got incredibly bad fills.

Example

Throughout the day, New York gold was trading very quietly, somewhere between 389 and 390 per ounce. When my friend Jack called his broker to buy one contract at the market. The price had been 389.10 for the last 5 minutes, so he naturally expected to get filled in that area. Jack has a real-time feed and chart program. Boy, was he surprised as he watched the screen when gold all of a sudden jumped to 389.90 for a second and then went back to 389.15. Guess who had just bought at 389.90? Jack! Not that the floor traders in Chicago are angels, but there seems to be a preponderance of locals attempting to pull *fast ones* in New York.

Day trading versus position trading

Choosing the right time frame is a another important aspect of trading. The two basic ways to trade are by day trading and position trading. Day trading means that trades are opened and closed on the same day. A position trade can be anything from 1 day (at least overnight) up to weeks or months.

Do not try to day trade using delayed data even though it is much cheaper than actual real-time data since there are no associated exchange fees. Even a 10-minute delay is unacceptable when one tries to take small profits throughout the day! Except for the rare, large moves, which may continue for hours, most short rallies last only 10-30 minutes. Any time delay on the feed will make it close to impossible to trade profitably.

Not all stocks and commodities are suitable for day trading. It is important to find the right mix of volatility and liquidity. A market has to move in order for you to make money. Stocks with small daily trading ranges or thinly traded commodities are unsuitable because the bid/ask spread will be prohibitively large in proportion to price activity.

Example

It is senseless to try to catch a stock's move of ° if the bid/ask spread is 3/8, since that 1/8 profit will be eaten up by commission.

Popular day trading commodity markets include:

- T-Bonds, CBOT (extremely good liquidity)
- S&P 500, CME (extremely good liquidity)
- Corn, CBOT (very good liquidity)
- Soybeans, CBOT (very good liquidity)
- Yen, German Mark, Swiss Franc, British Pound, IMM (good liquidity)

Intra-day time frames

About half of the professional traders interviewed by me for this book stated that novices should stay away from day trading altogether, while the other half did not share this view. Since traders must decide by themselves how to trade, a list of the pros and cons of each approach follows:

Day trading – Pros
- No overnight risk
- No weekend risk
- Lower commissions
- Ability to react to sudden moves

Day trading – Cons
- High software cost
- Expensive real-time data & exchange fees
- High proportion of commission expenses because of frequent trades
- Bad fills are proportionally more damaging
- Danger of overtrading
- Time consuming and potentially stressful

Position trading – Pros
- End-of-day is cheap and easily available
- Large variety of software
- Can easily be done in spare time
- Potentially very profitable when one catches big moves

Position trading – Cons

- Gaps can cause one to be stopped out far from the desired price
- Weekend risk
- Limit moves can keep one from exiting losing positions
- Margin requirements
- Large drawdowns

Hard & Software

Hardware

These days a private investor has computing power at his fingertips that just 10 years ago was limited to universities and major corporations. I remember when a 5 MB hard disk, a *Winchester drive*, seemed to offer an incredible amount of storage space. How could one ever fill it up? Back then a word processing program had 32KB and the Basic programming language was in ROM.

As I am writing this book (Spring 1997), 200Mhz Pentium computer systems are going for about $2000, but for most applications a 133-166Mhz system is more than adequate. More important than the processor speed, in my point of view, is the speed of the hard disk, amount of RAM and quality of the monitor.

A SCSI hard disk and controller will provide a noticeable performance increase over the cheaper IDE drives. It doesn't have to be the relatively expensive Ultra-Wide SCSI variety either, but if you have the money, get it. An incredibly fast SCSI hard disk was just introduced with a rotation speed of 10,000 rpm! Now we are talking fast access. The drive makes a sound like a jet engine while booting. Cheaper drives only spin at 5.400 rpm or less.

To run Windows 95 decently, currently the most popular operating system, requires at least 16MB to work. Another popular OS is Windows NT. It's a little more memory hungry and needs 32MB, or more, for satisfactory performance. With RAM prices being where they are right now, it make no sense to skimp on memory. Having enough memory keeps the computer from "swapping" information to disk, a process which is relatively time consuming. Even though I personally kind of like Apple computers, I would suggest that you stick to an IBM compatible system. Components and software for PC's are so plentiful that there is a solution for every need.

Choosing a high-quality monitor is important because that is what you will be spending a good deal of your time staring at. A speedy computer is a great thing, but if it takes 7 instead of 5 seconds to calculate something, it doesn't really make a big difference for most people. One the other hand, a bad monitor can cause blurry vision, headaches and take the fun out of charting.

What's the ideal size? A 17" currently offers the best price/performance ratio. It can easily support a display area of 1024 x 768, more than enough viewing several charts simultaneously. Twenty inch monitors are still quite expensive, although prices have come down recently. The problem with these monsters is that they eat up a great deal of desk space. I can't wait until those big, flat displays become available that have been promised for years.

Operating Systems

Windows 95 or Windows NT is the current operating system of choice. If you are still running Windows 3.1 or Windows for Workgroups– upgrade now! Windows 95 has better performance and is more suitable for multitasking (running several programs at once) than its predecessor. I also tend to adhere to the old adage *If it isn't broke, don't fix it*, but as far as computers are concerned, it also doesn't make much sense to work with an outdated system forever.

The real advantage of NT over 95 is its stability, file system and networking capabilities. Don't expect your programs to run considerably faster though. Older, 16 bit programs, may actually run somewhat slower under NT than under Windows 95. All developers of sophisticated trading systems I have met use NT. NT can make use of multiple processors (up to 4), speeding up extremely critical applications.

Charting Software

When it comes to chart software there are two major players: Equis International, makers of *MetaStock*, and Omega Research, makers of *TradeStation*, *SuperCharts* and *Wall Street Analyst*. News giant Reuters recently acquired Equis while Omega now has an alliance with Dow Jones/Markets. Other vendors of end-of-day programs include Aspen Research, Worden Brothers (*Telechart 2000*), Windows on Wall Street and many others.

The minimum set of features to look for in a charting program is:

- Display line, bar & candlestick charts
- Able to compress daily data to weekly and monthly charts
- Line studies: trendlines, Fibonacci retracements
- Indicators: relative strength index, simple moving average, stochastics, momentum, directional movement, on balance volume
- Easy way to update and maintain data

Top of the line chart programs like the ones from Omega Research and Equis will add dozens of more features, indicators and studies like:

- Point & Figure, Equivolume, Kagi and Renko charts
- Time Cycles
- Gann Lines
- Andrew's Pitchfork
- Weighted and exponential moving averages
- Automatic downloading of data and updating existing files
- Create custom indicators
- Scan entire directories for trading signals
- Automatic chart analysis by "wizards"

Figure 13. Candlestick chart of the Dow Jones Transportation Index. Note the top window with the directional movement indicator and the center window with a custom indicator. Both *MetaStock* and *TradeStation* can display over a dozen individual charts on one screen. MetaSock is a moderately priced end-of-day charting package featuring a wealth of indicators and tools for system design and testing.

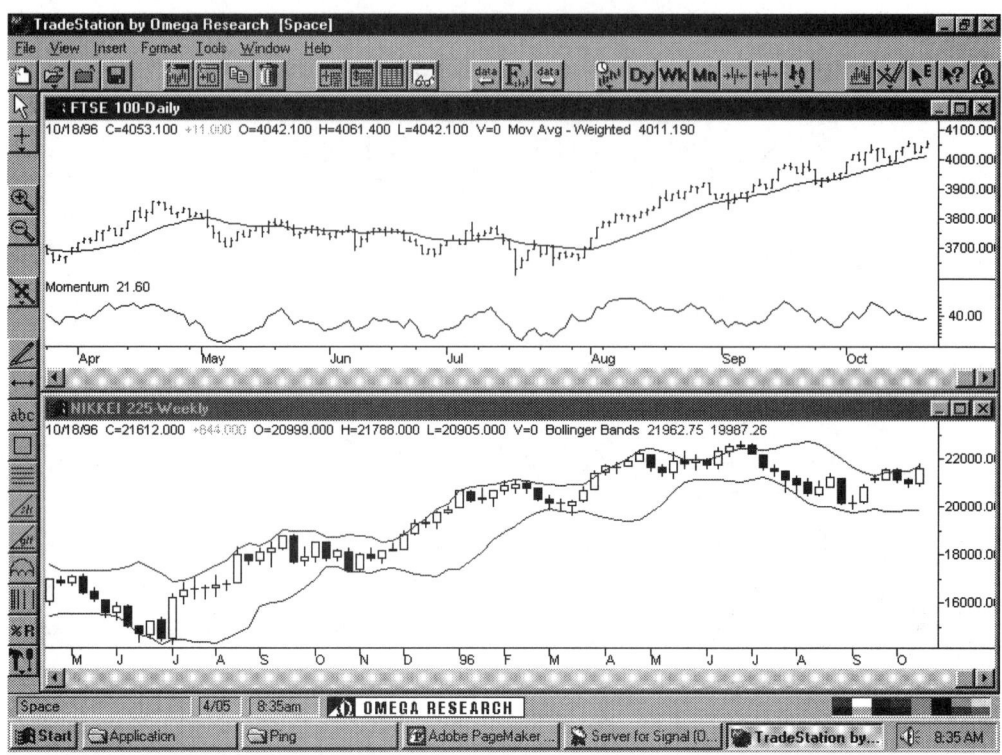

Figure 14. Screenshot of Omega TradeStation. Two individual windows display the FTSE and NIKKEI indexes. The NIKKEI chart is shown as a candlestick chart with Bollinger Bands, while the FTSE uses regular bars with the momentum indicator at the bottom of the chart. *TradeStation* is a high-end charting package featuring real-time intraday and end-of-day charting.

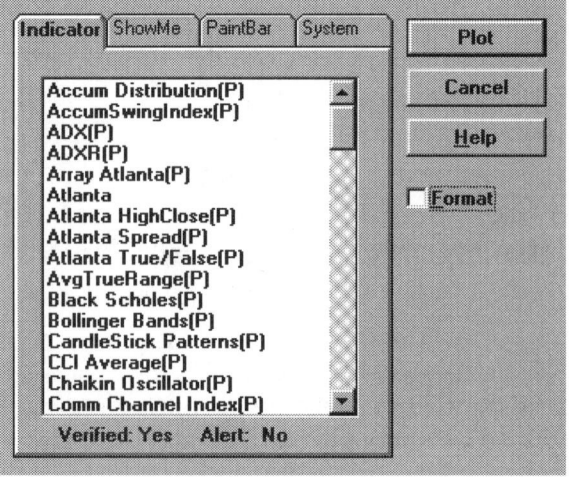

Figure 15. Screenshot of Omega TradeStation's indicator selection window. Both *TradeStation* and *MetaStock* have tons of indicators and let you create custom indicators as well.

Figure 16. This screenshot of *TeleChart 2000* by Worden Brothers is an example of an extremely low priced chart program ($29). Don't expect anything more than very basic chart functions with this DOS based program (the company is said to be releasing a windows version later in 1997).

Most important however, is the fact that high-end programs include a host of functions for system development and testing. User definable parameters will include important issues like commission, slippage, stops, profit targets and much more. Remember that hypothetical trading results will vary from actual trading, therefore it is important that the software can emulate as many real trading factors as possible.

The choice of software will be limited if one wants to go with real-time charting. Equis currently only offers a DOS based real-time package, *MetaStock* RT, but is said to be working on a new Windows version, due later in 1997. Look and feel of RT is that of the older, non-windows, versions of *MetaStock*. Omega has real-time versions of all three of their chart programs, with *Wall Street Analyst SE RT* (Special Edition Real Time) currently being offered for free by data vendor BMI.

Keep in mind that real-time software can get expensive. Omega's flagship program, *TradeStation*, costs about $2000, but offers an enormous amount of indicators, alerts, user-definable quote pages and functions for system design and testing. Real-time programs can be used, of course, for end of day analysis as well.

Figure 17. Screenshot of *TradeStation* with three intraday charts. They all represent the April 4, 1997 trading day of JP Morgan's stock. The chart on the left is (a portion) the day's trading using a tick chart (trade-by-trade). The graph on the top right is a 5-minute, and the lower right a 15-minute chart. Intraday charts exhibit the same characteristics and patterns as daily and weekly charts.

SYM: C Z7		VOL:	4260	CHG:		-26 TIME:	Dec30	
LST: s 2576		OI:	187375	HIGH:		2594 OPEN:	2594	
BID:		XL: CBT		LOW:		2574 OPEN2:		
ASK:		BASE: 1/8		PREV:		2604		

Detail Page: 1			Chicago Board of Trade (CBT)				Collection: SAMPLE	
SYMBOL	T	LAST	CHANGE	OPEN	HIGH	LOW	VOL	TIME TSIZE
N								
# Grains								
C H7	s	2582	-62	2630	2630	2580	95.2K	Dec30
C N7	s	2626	-46	2660	2660	2624	18.8K	Dec30
C Z7		2576	-26	2594	2594	2574	4.26K	Dec30
O H7	s	1526	-14	1520	1544	1520	2.26K	Dec30
O N7	s	1604	-10	1600	1610	1600	40	Dec30
S H7	s	6904	-62	6946	6946	6900	59.0K	Dec30
S N7	s	6874	-50	6900	6910	6870	10.5K	Dec30
SM H7	s	2196	-22	2204	2207	2183	4.65K	Dec30
SM N7	s	2129	-16	2136	2138	2115	553	Dec30
W H7	s	3820	-74	3886	3890	3814	16.6K	Dec30
W N7	s	3386	-30	3400	3410	3384	4.24K	Dec30

Fri 25 Apr 19:24:10   Limit Long   NODATA   S E 10 1107

Figure 17A. Screenshot of DBC's Signal for DOS real-time quote server. Almost all vendors permit the creation of customized quote pages.

Price Data

Obtaining price data is a prerequisite for using any chart program. Just a few years back it was common to pay $80-100 or more for daily updates of major markets. In addition, one had to make daily long distance calls to the data vendor's BBS (Bulletin Board System) to download the data. Collections of historic data on CD-ROM sometimes sold for several thousand dollars.

Nowadays huge amounts of historical prices are included free of charge when purchasing chart software. Expect to get between 5 to 25 years of stock, commodity, index and mutual fund history on CD-ROM with popular programs like *MetaStock*. We are talking massive amounts of data here, easily 100 MB or more. Not long ago this quantity of data was the realm of major financial institutions with computers the size of a living room. We really have come a long way, at least technically.

Data vendors and formats

End-of-day data

Here in the USA there are quite a few good sources for buying historic data and receiving daily updates. Some of the better known vendors include:

- Dial Data
- Tick Data (tick-by-tick historical data)
- Bridge Data (formerly Knight-Ridder)
- Reality Online (Reuters)
- CSI (Commodity Systems Inc.)
- Technical Tools
- Prophet
- Genesis

All of these companies offer historic data on CD-ROM, on a per quote and/ or monthly basis. Unless just a few items are needed, one is usually much better off by buying a CD instead of individual quotes. I do not recommend using AOL or CompuServe for more than updating just a few files daily, as their per quote charges are relatively high. It also may make sense to buy a new program just to get the included data CD-ROM. Some vendors have started charging a flat monthly fee for daily updates including unlimited history downloading.

Some issues to consider before deciding on a vendor:

· At what time is the data available for downloading?
· Is toll-free access to the BBS offered (extra charge?)
· Any discounts for getting data from the Internet?
· How long do downloads take?
· Is each category charged separately or can you mix and match?
· Are indices included free of charge?
· Does your chart program support the vendor's data format?
· Can your chart program download data or is it necessary to purchase separate software?

Real-time data

Real-time data is for the person who either does day-trade, or has the time to monitor markets throughout the day to find favorable entry points for position trades. Why would a position trader (a trader that keeps trades for days or weeks) need real-time data?

Example

A trading system might flash a buy signal after scanning today's prices. Instead of just entering the market at the open the next day, a trader might know from experience that it is likely that a better price could be obtained by waiting a while after the markets open. This approach only makes sense for professional or semi-professional traders, as the added expenses for real-time data, exchange fees and intraday software will outweigh the benefits, if one only trades once or twice per month.

Real-time and delayed data is received tick-by-tick. The software running on the PC collects this data to generate 5, 10, 15, 30 or whatever minute charts. Some programs only support these common time frames, while others are more flexible, permitting charting of any time frame. In fact, some traders deliberately use a 14-minute chart instead of a 15-minute one, since the majority of traders only use obvious time frames. The trader with the 14-minute chart could have a slight advantage (remember, seconds do count when day-trading) when certain chart patterns occur.

Omega *TradeStation* adds something called tick charts to regular, time-based charts. Instead of waiting for a given amount of time to pass before a new bar is drawn on the screen, the specified amount of ticks becomes the determining factor. A 10-tick chart will display a new bar after 10 prices have crossed the line, regardless of the amount of time that has passed. It could take a few seconds or hours. Tick charts are an interesting alternative to normal time-based charts.

Delayed data (usually 10-30 minutes, depending on the exchange) is offered much cheaper than the real-time variety, since no exchange fees are levied. The CME (Chicago Mercantile Exchange) currently charges $70 per month, while the Mid-Am exchange is a real bargain at only $7 per month. Do not try to day trade with delayed data, it's like driving down the highway with one eye closed. Delayed intraday prices can be useful for designing and testing day-trading systems however.

Major real-time data vendors

- Dow Jones/Telerate
- Reuters
- BMI
- Signal
- S&P Comstock
- FutureSource
- DTN
- CQG

Note

BMI and Signal are both owned by the same company, Data Broadcasting Corporation. The level of service and pricing vary somewhat.

Real-time data can be received the following ways. Check with each vendor to see which options are available:

- Cable TV
- Satellite
- FM
- Leased Line

Cable is usually the preferred way to go. Cable is most immune to weather related disturbances and supports a high bandwidth (speed at which data can be transmitted). Furthermore, almost every home or apartment already has cable TV. The channels used by vendors to send data are usually ESPN, CNN and AMC. Traders living in remote areas might have to settle for the satellite dish. Be prepared to spend an entire day setting the system up. Not only will you have to assemble the whole thing, but position and fine-tune it as well. On top of that, you will have to run the coax cable into your house, somewhere, which means drilling a long hole. I kind of had fun setting the system up, but then again I'm a sucker for any high-tech gadget! It was somehow exhilarating when the first quotes appeared on my screen. Kind of like connecting with the mother ship for the first time.

Try to choose a vendor whose feed is supported by a wide range of software products. Windows based chart programs are generally much more powerful and easier to use than the ones running under DOS. Most Window programs support DDE, which lets one paste data to an Excel spreadsheet, where further calculations can be performed in real-time.

```
15:28:00 [#STOCKS] OUTPERFORMERS: HMOS, ENVIRONMENTALS, SEMICONDUCTORS, INSURERS.
16:13:00 [#TECH ROSS] ROSS SYSTEMS EARNS 4 CENTS/SHARE IN Q2 VS YR-AGO 2-CENT LOSS.
16:15:00 [#GEN #STOCKS] THURSDAY'S WINNERS: THE DOLLAR, LONDON STOCKS, PEPSI.
16:16:00 [#STOCKS] RUSSELL 2000 INDEX OF SMALL STOCKS DECLINED 0.1% FOR DAY.
16:18:00 [#STOCKS] OUTPERFORMERS:  HMOS, ENVIRONMENTALS, CASINOS, INSURERS.
16:19:00 [#STOCKS INBR VST] THURSDAY'S LOSERS: INBRAND CORP., VANSTAR, DOW INDUSTRIALS.
16:20:00 [#STOCKS] UNDERPERFORMERS:  RETAILERS, INTERNETS, SOFTWARES, DRUGS.
16:21:00 [#TECH] NASDAQ COMPOSITE CLOSES DOWN 0.7% AS ORACLE, INBRED TUMBLE.
16:22:00 [#EARN ERTS] ELECTRONIC ARTS EARNS 66 CENTS IN Q3 VS YR-AGO 54 CENTS.
16:23:00 [#STOCKS #NET AOL CNWK XCIT] NET STOCKS END MIXED; AOL, CNET, EXCITE FALL...
16:24:00 [#STOCKS] NYSE DECLINERS LED ADVANCERS 14-11 ON RECORD VOLUME.
16:25:00 [#STOCKS] DOW CLOSES DOWN 94.28, OR 1.4%, TO 6755.75 AFTER HITTING 6900.
16:26:00 [#TECH #EARN SYBS] SYBASE EARNS 7 CENTS/SHARE IN Q4 VS. YR-AGO 8 CENTS.
16:28:00 [#TECH #NET #EARN WALL] WALL DATA EARNS 28 CENTS/SHARE IN Q4 VS YR-AGO 25 CENTS
16:30:00 [#STOCKS] AMEX COMPOSITE FALLS 0.2% TO CLOSE AT 589.69.
16:31:00 [#STOCKS] PSE TECHNOLOGY INDEX FALLS 0.4%; NASDAQ 100 FALLS 1.4%.
16:32:00 [#STOCKS] NYSE COMPOSITE FALLS 0.9% TO CLOSE AT 409.15.
16:33:00 [#STOCKS] DOW TRANSPORTS CLOSE 0.3% LOWER; DOW UTILITIES CLOSE 0.2% LOWER.
16:35:00 [#HEALTH #EARN SGI] SILICON GRAPHICS LOSES 7 CENTS A SHARE IN Q2 AFTER CHARGES.
16:43:00 [#EARN SYMC] SYMANTEC EARNS 25 CENTS/SHARE IN Q3 VS OPERATING NET OF 1 CENT.
17:11:00 [#TECH #NET AOL] AOL SAYS IT IS COOPERATING WITH ATTORNEYS GENERA.
17:26:00 [#TECH #LEISURE ERTS] ELECTRONIC ARTS Q3 NET $0.66/SHR VS $0.54.
17:46:00 [#GEN] ARMY STRIKES REBELS IN RWANDA; HUNDREDS REPORTED KILLED.
```

Figure 18. Sample of headline news optionally available when subscribing to a data service. With some services one can opt to read the entire story, while others only offer headlines.

The three most common end-of-day data formats

MetaStock

The most widely supported data format is probably Equis' *MetaStock*, even though Equis itself was never in the data vending business. *MetaStock* is based on a file format originally created by (the now defunct) *Computrac*, creator of the very first technical analysis program for a personal computer.

MetaStock files generally either use a 5 or 7 field format. Five fields can store the date, high, low, close and volume, while the seven field variety stores date, open, high, low, volume and open interest (futures only, otherwise zero). If compatibility with other programs is an issue, be sure to select a vendor that supports *MetaStock* and/or has software for converting data back and forth. There is practically no program of any significance that cannot read the *MetaStock* format.

CSI – Commodity Systems

CSI uses their own proprietary format, which is supported by most major programs. The CSI downloading software has the ability to update *MetaStock* files along with their own format.

Technical Tools

This company has been providing data for a long time and was once owned by famous trader Ed Seykota. The TechTool format is widely supported, but their downloading software can convert to ASCII, CSI, *MetaStock* and more, if needed.

Why are there so many competing formats? Why not use plain ASCII (text) instead? Wouldn't this make things much easier? Unfortunately, not. ASCII files take up a lot more space. In addition, all vendors would have to agree on a common record layout, something that is just as unlikely as everbody deciding on the same format.

The importance of clean data

Clean data refers to data that has as few errors as possible. Errors include the following: misplaced decimal points (9700 instead of 97.00), open or close prices that are outside of the high-low range and prices that are just total nonsense. Bad data does not even have to be the vendor's fault. The exchanges themselves sometimes transmit bad data!

A majority of obvious errors are easily spotted. Each vendor handles error correction differently. Some will periodically send out corrections lists, where the user has to manually edit prices, while others have software that perform automatic error correction while updating files. Why clean data is so important will be apparent in a second. I have been involved in the development of trading systems where we found out that one and the same system would show vastly different performance depending on the data vendor!

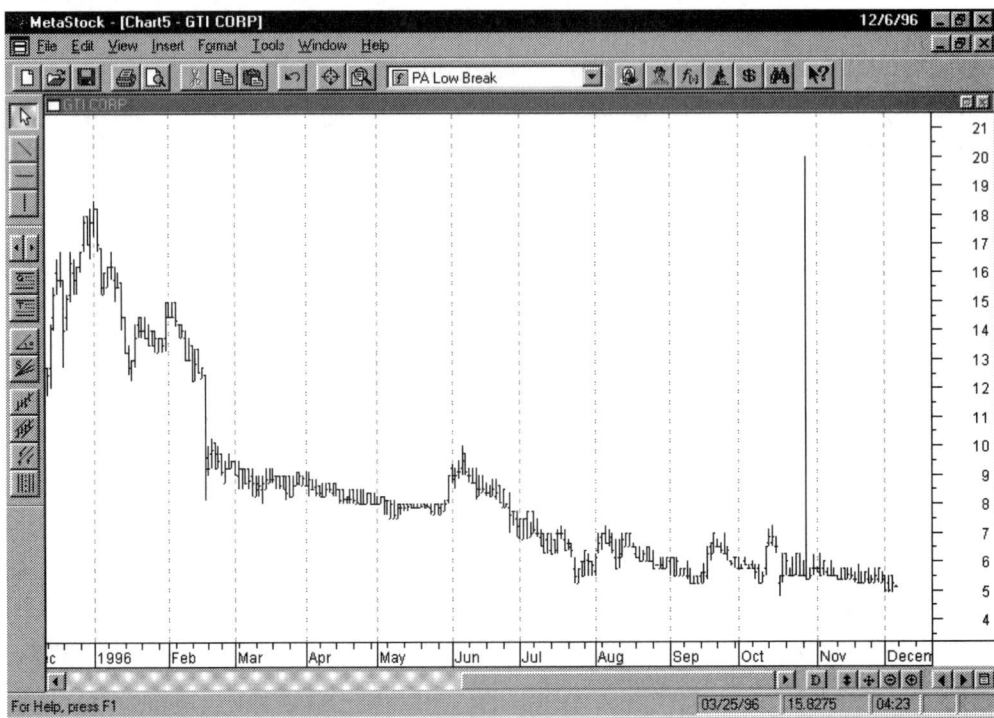

Figure 19. Note the daily bar towards the end of October which is obviously incorrect. Unfortunately not all errors are spotted this easily.

Example

A short-term trend following system, using data vendor A's prices would generate a 24% profit. The exact same system, using the same stocks and dates from vendor B however, would show a 2% loss! The differences are not always this extreme, but can be quite eye opening.

Many professional traders therefore subscribe to two or more services. The data is constantly cross-checked to insure the highest quality possible. This applies to real-time, as well as end of day data.

How much history

Novices always wonder about much price history they should get. It all depends. A trader who just performs basic technical analysis, but does not venture into system development might only need a few years of the markets that are followed. Market behavior changes over time, so charts that are more than 10 years old may not be very good in relating to current market conditions.

The point is to have samples of as wide a range of market conditions as possible. What does Delta's stock look like when it is in a trading range? What are the wildest swings Crude Oil can demonstrate? What does it look like when a mutual fund really takes off? Having seen charts with various market conditions makes it easier to spot patterns in the present. In addition I would suggest to have 10 or more years of all major indices in order to keep track of long-term trends.

A system developer on the other hand will need substantially more historic data. Without getting into details at this point, the reason is that mechanical trading systems need to be tested for performance with a set of data that includes as many market phases as possible. Systems that have profit potential then need to face the *out of sample* challenge. Out of sample refers to a set of data that the system has not experienced during the development stage. Ten years of history is probably the least amount of data a system developer needs.

Example

A simple trend following system shows acceptable results when being tested with Corn prices from 1985 to 1990. How does the same system perform when data from 1991 to 1996 is entered? If the results are much worse the system can be considered flawed.

Preparing for the First Trade

Plan the trade - trade the plan

The most important thing a new trader has to get accustomed to do is to prepare a trade plan. Nobody goes on vacation without planning the route, getting plane tickets and making hotel reservations. Trading is no different. One has to know in advance the kind of trade one is looking for, expected duration, risk/reward ratio and under which circumstances the trade is exited.

An entry could be based on prices making new highs or the violation of a trendline. An exit can be based on a stop-loss order being triggered or the reaching of a profit-target. The point here is that the strategy, entry and exit, must be defined in *advance*. There is nothing more deadly than simply trading on the spur of the moment (there are a few great traders who simply use their instincts, but those instincts were usually honed by years of experience) and having a mental stop. A mental stop is an order to close your position at a price that is only in your head, not in the market.

Example

Let's assume you bought IBM (insert your favorite stock here) at 120 and you are willing to stick with it if it goes down to 110, but not lower. Your assumption is that if IBM goes below110 the general outlook may have changed and it is better to get out. Now, let's assume that with your mental stop in place, IBM suddenly starts drifting slowly towards the 110 mark, hovers there for a day or two and then suddenly closes 5 dollars lower at 105. At this point two things are likely to happen: either you call your broker to sell at the open the next day, in which case you will have lost 5 dollars more per share than you were originally willing to risk (in reality there is a chance that the stock will open even lower, increasing your loss). Or you will begin to rationalize that this can surely only be a small correction and that prices will bounce back shortly. After all, you did your homework, examined the charts and IBM is definitely ready for a serious rally.

Over the course of the next few days IBM goes up to 107, retreats to 105 and then goes down to 102. You are now minus 18 per share, 80% more than you were actually willing to risk. Since nobody likes to admit a mistake, 102 begins to look cheap and you decide to buy another 100 shares, reasoning that you now have evened out your purchase price to 111. But now IBM seriously starts to tumble since Howard, Smith and Kapunzky (insert your favorite investment bank here) just lowered their earnings estimate, and major stop-loss orders were triggered when prices dipped below 100! The point illustrated here is that stops **must be in the market, not in the head**. A mental stop is a no-no. In fact, a stop should always be placed at the same time a trade is entered. Not "let's see how things develop and then I'll call my broker with the stop."

One might argue that everything could have worked out just as well, even without a stop. IBM rebounded, went up to 130, and all 200 shares were sold for a handsome profit. Sure, anything can happen, but preservation of capital is priority one. Traders can, and do, have strings of losing trades. By getting out of losing trades with a small, predefined loss one is able to stay in the game. It's the few, big losers that wipe out most novices.

Try keeping a *trading log*, making notes of each trade stating why it was entered, how much was risked and the final result. This way one can always go back at a later time, when a similar trade opportunity arises, to compare, evaluate and modify the strategy.

Every trader must make a habit of entering all trades into an *order log*. An order log keeps track of the date, time, number of shares or contracts, ticket number, price filled and stop-loss order. Brokers can and do make mistakes. It is really only a matter of time until something gets messed up, like the broker bought the wrong amount of shares, misunderstood the stop, account number, or whatever. Since conversations between a broker and client are taped, knowing the exact date and time at which an order was placed can help straighten things out.

Stocks, futures, foreign exchange, options and mutual funds all have different characteristics and risk levels. Decisions have to be made as to which instruments within a market are to be traded, as there are big differences in liquidity and volatility between members of the same family. It would be wrong to say that all stocks are safer to trade than futures, or that mutual funds are necessarily safer than stocks.

The average trading range is another important factor to consider. Even markets with relatively low volatility may be unsuitable for a given trader. Often a good commodity for futures traders to start out with is corn. Sure, corn is (usually) much less volatile than, say, orange juice, but 3 or 4-cent moves in a day are very common. A one cent move of the Chicago Board of Trade (CBOT) corn contract is worth $50, so an average range of $150-200 might be too high a risk for a trader who doesn't want to risk more than $100 per trade. A tight stop-loss order could be used to decrease the amount at risk, but this will probably result in trades being stopped out too frequently. A solution to the problem could be to find an alternate exchange with smaller contract sizes (such as the Mid America Exchange) or consider a different market, such as Eurodollars.

These observations apply to stocks as well. A $10 stock with a trading range of 1 dollar increases or decreases its value by 10%. A $50 stock with the same 1 dollar average trading range fluctuates by only 2%. Assuming you had $1000 to play with, and you had the choice of making $1 per share with either stock, which one would you buy? The answer is the $10 stock, since one could buy 100 shares, making $100 in profits. With the same $1000 one could only buy 20 shares of the $50 stock, resulting in a profit of only $20. Evaluating risk/reward ratios is paramount for successful trading.

PART II

Chart Basics

Chart styles

In order to perform any kind of technical analysis it is obviously necessary to convert raw price data into a graphical representation. Some gifted individuals are able to automatically visualize large amounts of numbers, but most of us aren't this lucky. The following popular chart styles are supported by most charting packages.

The Bar Chart

Bar charts are the most popular and widely used chart type. They are used to represent the high, low and close or open, high, low and close. A bar chart can, of course, be used with any time frame: 5-minute, 30-minute, daily, weekly, monthly or yearly. The top of the vertical bar is the high, the bottom the low, the short horizontal line to the left (if present) the open, and the line to the right the close. A good thing about bar charts is that one can immediately gauge a security's price range. As mentioned earlier in the book, a good trader always is aware of trading ranges. Chart formations, like triangles, flags and so forth, are also more easily identified with bar charts than with other chart types.

Figure 20. Bar chart segment. Note that each bar has a short line to the left (open) and to the right (close).

The Line Chart

While bar charts offer insight into all aspects of price activity, some analysts only look at the most important price, the close. Thus, a line chart is constructed by simply connecting closing prices.

If there is only one price to work with, a line chart will be the only choice. Examples are No-Load funds and economic time series like interest rates, producer price index and unemployment rates.

Figure 21. Line chart of the Janus Overseas mutual fund. Mutual funds only have one daily price, the NAV (net asset value), so only line charts can be utilized.

The Candlestick Chart

Japanese candlestick charts became popular in the West around 1991 with the publication of a book called *Japanese Candlestick Charting Techniques*, New York Institute of Finance, by Steve Nison. As candlesticks are not only a way of charting, but also incorporate *pattern analysis*, this section will be somewhat lengthier.

70

Candlestick charts require the open, high, low and close prices for construction. The high, low and close alone are not sufficient. There are three basic types of candlesticks: the black body, white body and cross. A black body occurs when the close is lower than the open. A white body is drawn when the close is higher than the open. With a cross the open and close are equal. Based on these basic candle types the Japanese have defined a complex array of patterns, depending on factors like body size and shadow length. A shadow is the thin line extending to the high or low. A detailed explanation for each pattern goes well beyond the scope of this book, so we are sticking to the most popular ones.

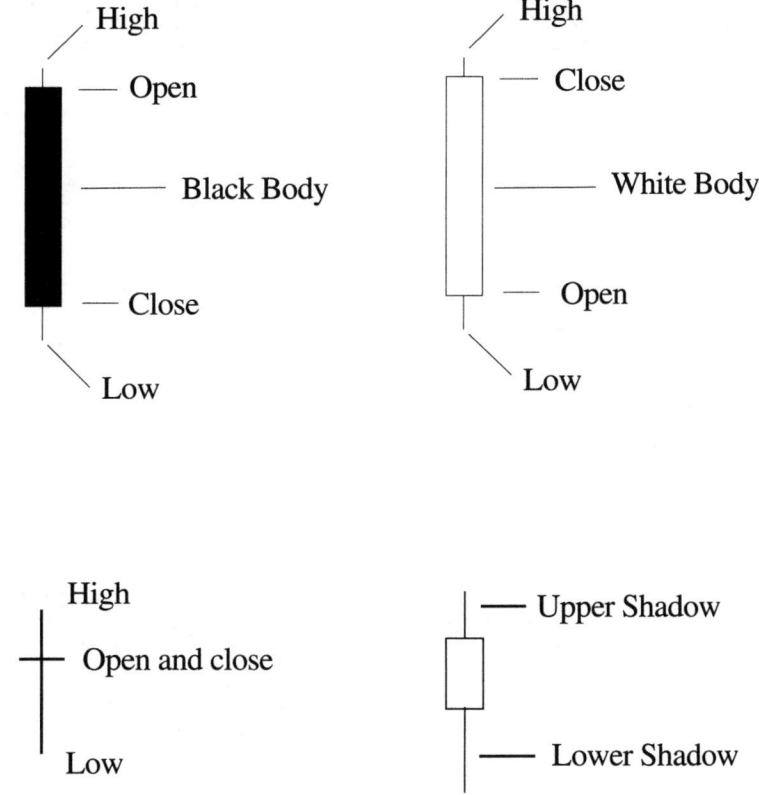

Figure 22. Basic candle types. Black body, white body and cross. Note that the line extending from the body to the high is called upper shadow and the line extending from the body to the low is called the lower shadow.

What candlestick charting and analysis boils down to is pattern recognition. History is known to repeat itself and the markets are no different. Thus, certain formations have been proven to have a high predictive value. Patterns can consist of one, or the combination of two or more candles. A selection of principal candlestick patterns and their interpretation follows:

- Bullish Engulfing
- Bearish Engulfing
- Dark Cloud Cover
- Hammer - Hanging Man
- Two Crows
- Piercing Line
- Spinning Top
- Meeting Line
- Shooting Star

Bullish Engulfing Pattern & Bearish Engulfing Pattern

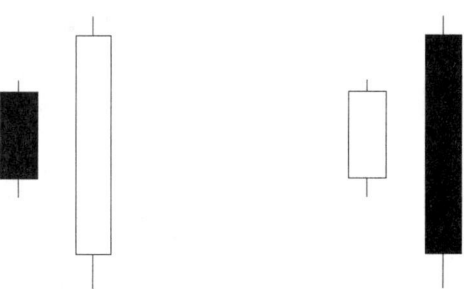

Figure 23. Bullish and Bearsh Engulfing Patterns.

These two formations are called engulfing patterns since the right candle's thick part (the "real body") engulfs the prior candle's real body. A Bullish Engulfing Pattern gives a good signal when it appears after a downtrend and prices are at an important support level, or other indicators are flashing buy signals as well. The longer the white candle and the smaller the black body, the better the signal. A Bearish Engulfing Pattern is the exact opposite of the bullish engulfing pattern. It warns of a possible downturn when it appears as prices hit important resistance levels, or other indicators are flashing sell signals as well.

Dark Cloud Cover

The Dark Cloud Cover has similar implications as the bearish engulfing pattern. The black body's close must be under the white body's midpoint and its open has to be above the white candle's high. The pattern should appear at tops in order to give good signals.

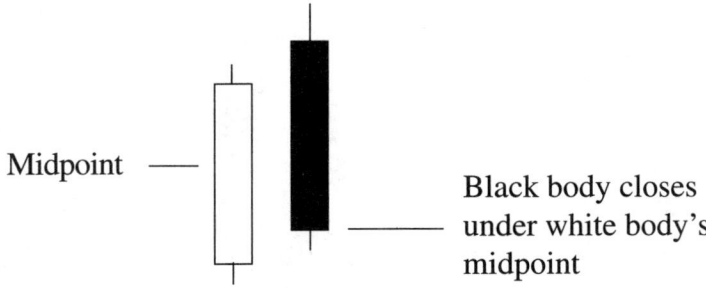

Midpoint ——

Black body closes under white body's midpoint

Figure 24. Bearish Dark Cloud Cover pattern.

Hammer - Hanging Man

The Hammer and Hanging Man patterns are basically identical, also known as "Umbrella lines." Which name is used depends on the position within the chart. When it appears after a prolonged downtrend the hammer signals a bullish reversal. "The market is hammering out a base." The hanging man is an umbrella line that appears after a prolonged uptrend. As the name implies, the hanging man is a bearish pattern. With either the Hammer or Hanging Man the lower shadow must be at least twice as long as the real body. There is little or no upper shadow. Although the body can be white or black the signals seem to be better with black bodies.

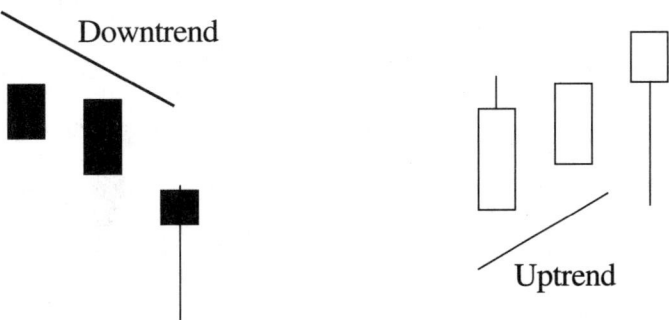

Downtrend

Uptrend

Figure 25. Bullish Hammer in a downtrend (left) and bearish Hanging Man in an uptrend (right).The candles before the Hammer/Hanging Man are for illustration only and do not have to be of the same size or shape.

73

Two Crows

Also sometimes called Upside Gap Two Crows, this pattern is bearish. After a long white body there are two black bodies of which the first one gaps above the white candle. The second black body opens even higher, but closes even lower than the first black body. This pattern is not too common but is usually very reliable.

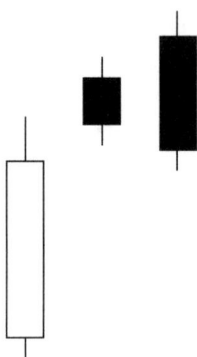

Figure 26. Bearish Two Crows pattern.

Morning Star - Evening Star

These reversal patterns consist of three candles. The Morning Star is a bullish reversal pattern. When it appears in a downtrend it signals that dawn (higher prices) is near. Note the gaps between the star (which can be black or white) and the candles to the left and right. The evening star warns of darkness setting in (for prices that is), and should appear in an uptrend. Note that gaps (price jumps) must be present between the middle candle and the candles to either side.

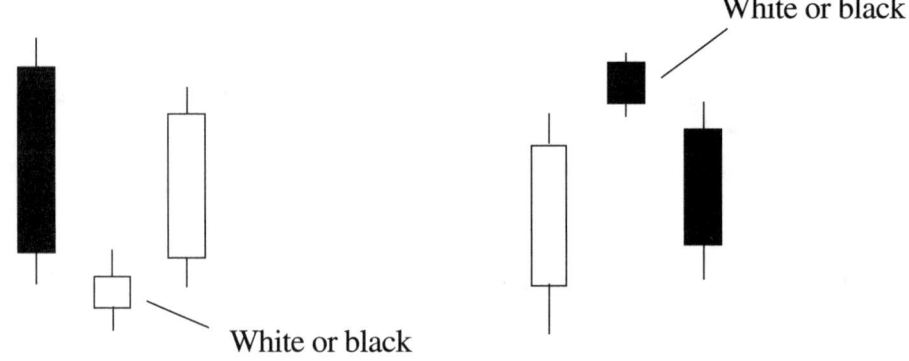

Figure 27. Bullish Morning Star (left) and bearish Evening Star (right).

74

Meeting Line

The meeting line formation is also know as *Counter Attack Lines*. There are two varieties, bearish and bullish. Two candles of different color both have the same close. Implication: the strength of preceeding move has diminished.

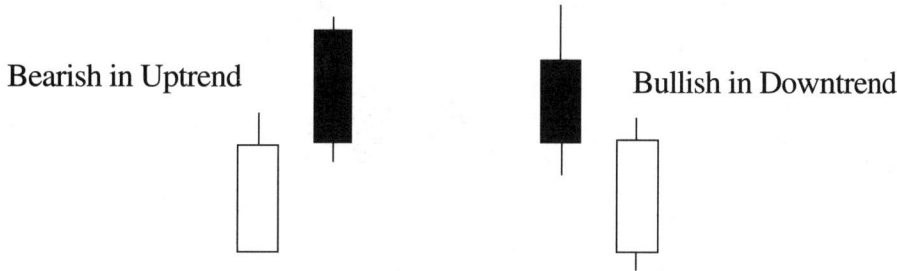

Bearish in Uptrend   Bullish in Downtrend

Figure 28. Bearish and Bullish Meeting Lines.

Shooting Star

A Shooting Stars is a reversal pattern. A star in general is a small real body that gaps away from the previous candle (as with the morning and evening star patterns). A shooting star is a star with a very long upper shadow and a very short, or absent, lower shadow. Shooting stars often call market tops with uncanny accuracy.

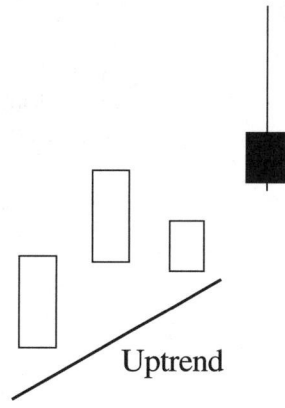

Uptrend

Figure 29. Shooting Star with a small black body after an uptrend often warns of an imminent reversal.

It is important to note that the occurrence of a candlestick pattern, by itself, is not necessarily a signal to trade. Rather, patterns should be used in conjunction with other indicators, studies and charting techniques. A nice size bullish engulfing pattern after a period of consolidation, along with, say, increasing momentum, is of much greater importance than the same pattern appearing by itself. Bear in mind that candlestick analysis contains a high degree of subjectivity, possibly more than conventional technical analysis. What one trader sees as a major bullish engulfing pattern may be of no significance to another. When is a "long shadow" really long? Also, some patterns may work more reliably with certain markets than with others. This could be due to the fact that each market has a specific "personality," formed by the collective psychology of its participants.

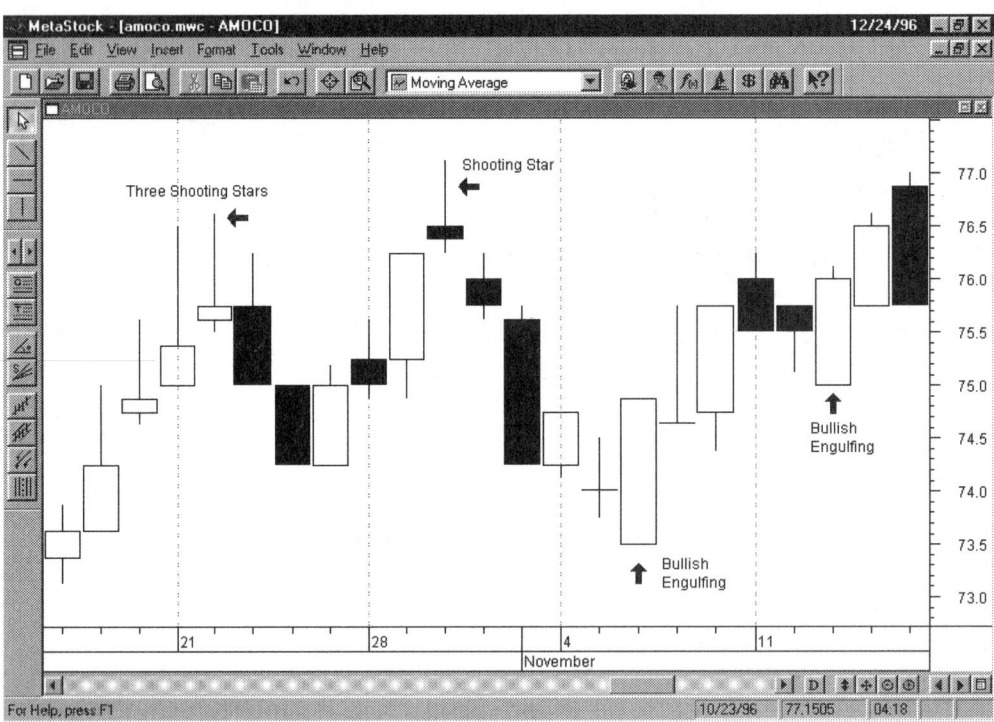

Figure 30. Chart of Amoco with several candlestick patterns. Note the three shooting stars to the left of the chart. Although Shooting Stars may, by definition, have a white or black body, the ones with a black body seem to be more reliable.

The Kagi, Renko and Three Line Break Charts

Besides candlesticks, Japanese analysts use chart styles called Kagi, Renko and Three Line Break charts. Analyst Steve Nison is again responsible for making these techniques known to the west. Details on the subject can be found in his book *Beyond Candlesticks*, Wiley, 1994, available through Traders Press.

Kagi charts display a series of connecting vertical lines where the thickness and direction of the lines are dependent on the price action. If closing prices continue to move in the direction of the prior vertical Kagi line, that line is extended. But, if the closing price reverses by a predetermined "reversal" amount, a new Kagi line is drawn in the next column in the opposite direction. An interesting aspect of the Kagi chart is that when closing prices penetrate the prior column's high or low, the thickness of the Kagi line changes. Kagi charts are an interesting way to view the underlying supply and demand of a market. A series of thick lines shows that demand is exceeding supply, a series of thin lines shows that supply is exceeding demand. A series of alternating thick and thin lines show that the market may be in a relative state of equilibrium (supply equals demand). The most common trading technique is to buy when the Kagi line changes from thin to thick, and sell when the Kagi line changes from thick to thin.

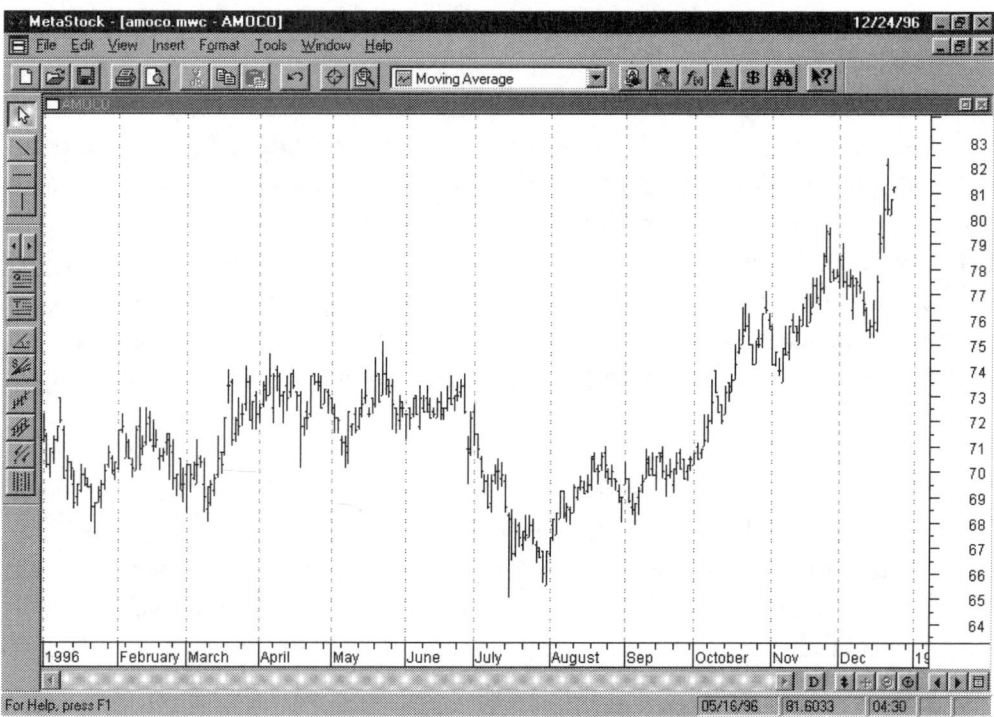

Figure 30. The following Kagi, Renko and Three Line Break charts are all based on Amoco, here shown as a regular bar chart.

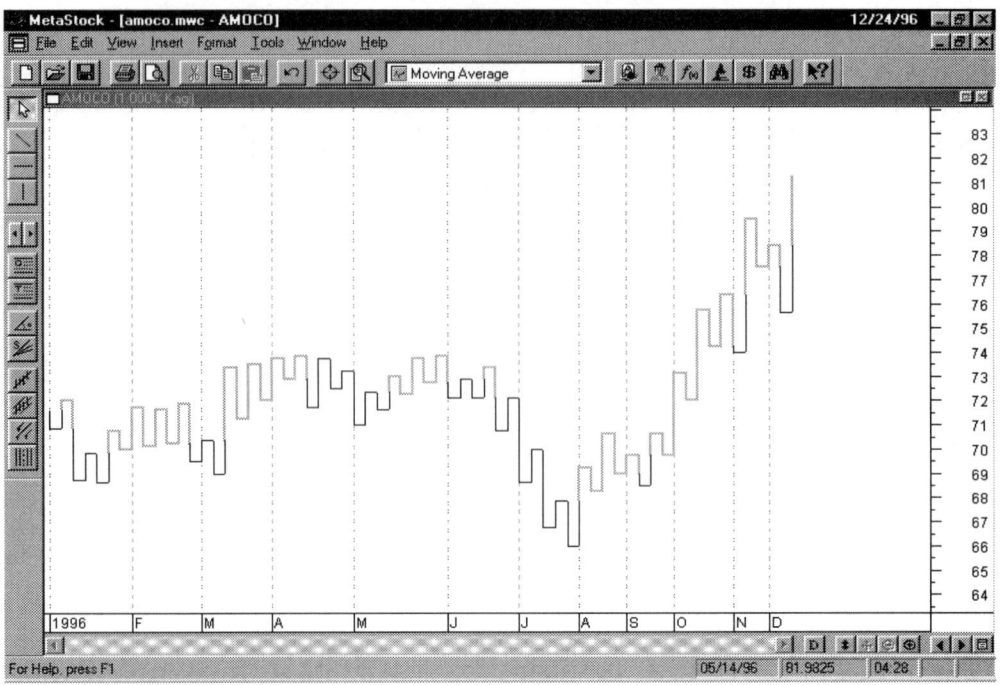

Figure 31. Kagi chart of Amoco using a one point reversal.

Renko charts are similar to Three Line Break charts, except that in a Renko chart a line is drawn in the direction of the prior move only if a fixed amount, the box size, has been exceeded. These lines are sometimes referred to as bricks. The bricks are always equal in size. For example, in a five-unit Renko chart, a 20 point rally is displayed as four equally sized, five-unit high Renko bricks. To draw Renko bricks, today's close is compared with the previous brick's high and low, white or black. When the closing price rises above the top of the previous brick by the box size or more, one or more white bricks of equal height are drawn in the next column. If the closing price falls below the bottom of the previous brick by the box size or more, one or more black bricks of equal height are drawn in the next column.

Basic trend reversals are signaled with the emergence of a white or black brick. A new white brick indicates the beginning of a new uptrend. A new black brick indicates the beginning of a new downtrend. Since the Renko chart is a trend following technique, there will be times when the market induces whipsaws. However, a trend following technique is intended to allow traders to ride on the major portion of the trend. Since a Renko chart isolates the underlying trends by filtering out the minor ups and downs, Renko charts are excellent for helping determine support and resistance levels.

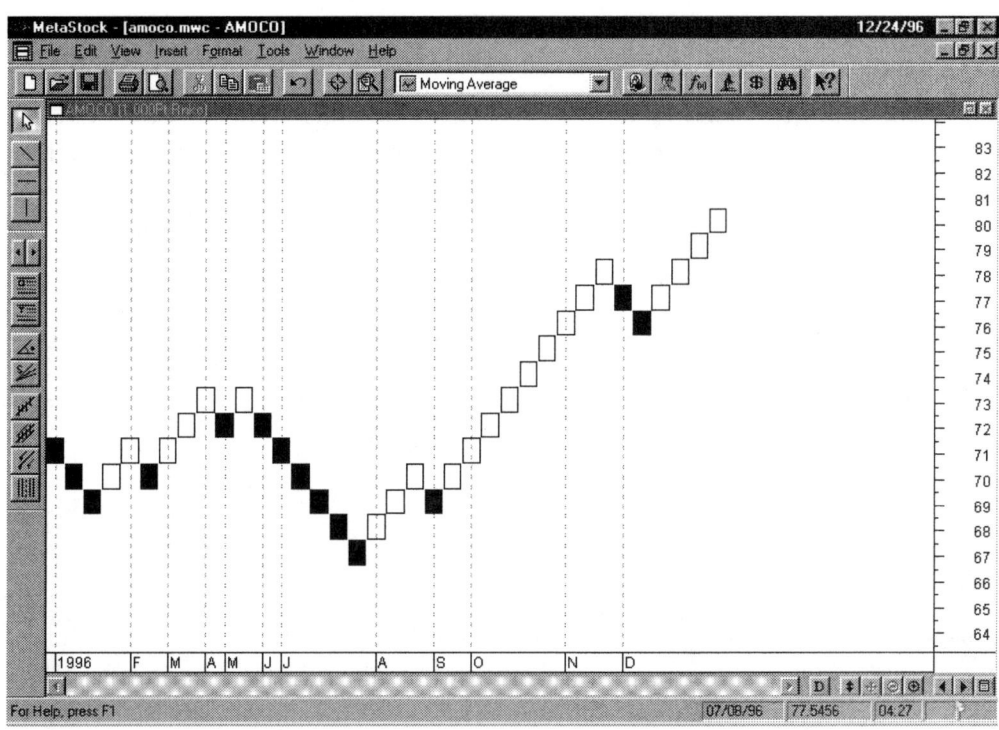

Figure 32. Renko chart of Amoco using a box size of one.

Figure 33. Three Line Break chart of Amoco using a one line parameter.

Point and Figure Chart

Point and figure charts look very different from conventional line and bar charts. Besides the appearance, the major difference is that time is completely ignored, resulting in a more compressed format. Only price changes are recorded. Point and figure charts are thus able to present a much larger amount of price history on a chart than any other chart style.

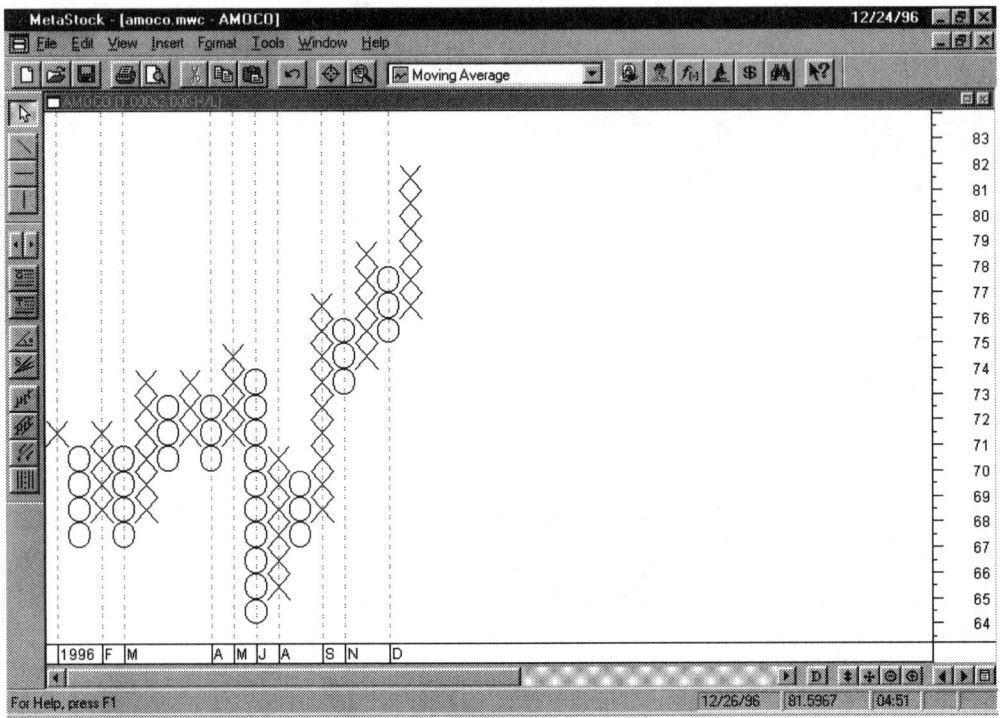

Figure 34. Point and Figure chart of Amoco, using the same data as the previous Kagi, Renko and Three Line Break charts. Parameters used were: box size 1, reversal amount 3.

Note the alternating columns of X's and O's (that's O not zero). X's represent rising prices and O's falling prices. What is the advantage of a point and figure chart? Some analysts feel that buy and sell signals are more precise and easier to spot. Also, there is more flexibility in constructing the chart as the user can define the box and reversal size, two parameters that govern the chart's sensitivity. Point and figure charts can be used with intraday or end of day data.

Now that we have mentioned the advantages of P&F charting, let's briefly look at how charts are constructed. If your chart program supports P&F charts the only factors you will have to worry about are the box and reversal sizes. The box size is the value assigned to each box on the chart. Thus, a box could have a value of $1, $2.50 or 10 cents, depending on the market being analyzed. Generally speaking, the larger the box value, the less sensitive the chart becomes, but the value should always be in proportion to the market. A $1 to $2 box size for gold would be appropriate, just like a 50 cent box size for a stock trading at around $30. But there are no hard rules to follow so just go ahead and experiment until you find what suits the particular situation best. By default most chart programs use a one point box value and three box reversal.

The reversal size defines the number of boxes that the market has to retrace in order to cause a switch to the next column to the right. A reversal size of one means that the market has to retrace only one full box to start a new column to the right. With a three box reversal the market must retrace three full boxes before a new column is started. It should be obvious that a small reversal size will result in more columns being drawn. By adjusting and tweaking these two parameters a trader is able to come up with a chart suiting his specific requirements, something no other chart style is able to do.

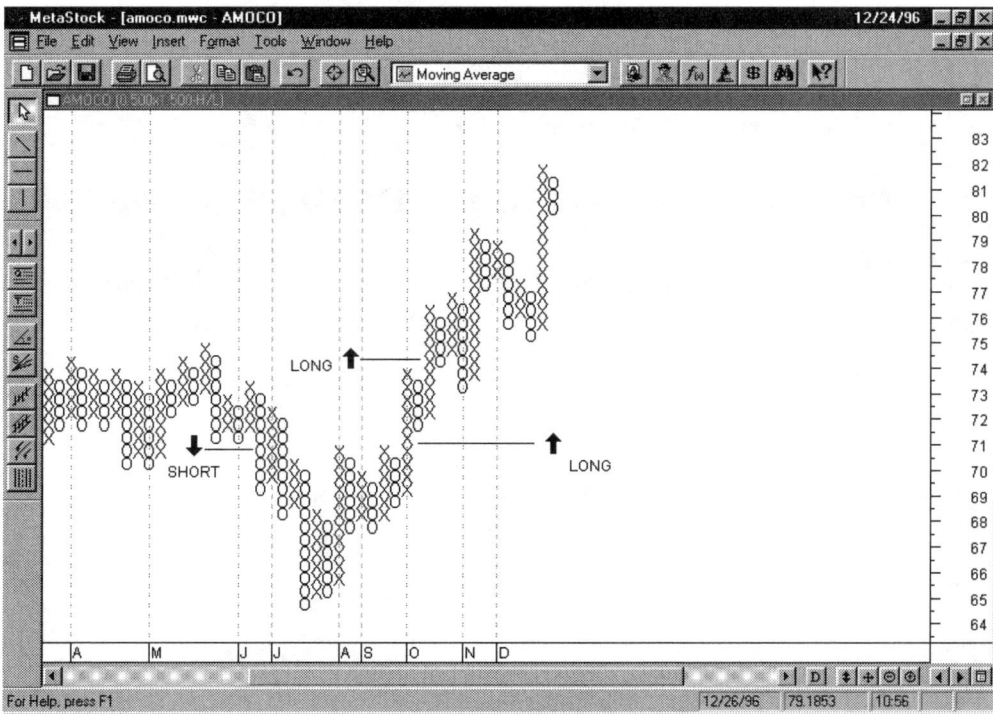

Figure 35. Point and Figure chart of Amoco, using a box size of .5 and reversal amount of 3. The classic way to trade point and figure charts is to go long when an X column exceeds the previous X column by one X to the upside and go short when a O column exceeds the previous O column by one O to the downside.

Note

Gaps have been traditionally ignored with point and figure charts since, according to purists, all box spaces must be filled. But some analysts do leave blank boxes when gaps occur, since they feel that they indicate important support and resistance points.

The Equivolume Chart

The Equivolume chart aims to combine the important information contained in trading volume with the price chart itself. This is cleverly achieved by widening the high-low line to a box with the width depending on trading volume. This method was developed by Richard Arms Jr. and is explained in detail in his book, *Volume Cycles in the Stock Market: Market Timing through Equivolume Charting* (Homewood, IL: Dow Jones-Irwin, 1983) available through Traders Press.

Short and wide boxes (i.e., small change in price combined with heavy volume) tend to be seen at turning points while tall and narrow boxes (i.e., large change combined with low volume) are more likely to be seen during continuing moves. The more volume in a top or bottom consolidation, the larger the ensuing move is likely to be. Volume is directly observable on an Equivolume chart by noting the overall width of the consolidation.

Figure 36. Equivolume chart of Amoco.

Indicators

Indicators are probably the most powerful tools that a trader has at his disposal. They are mathematical calculations that can be applied to one or more price fields, volume, open interest or a combination of these. It is even possible to apply one indicator onto another! The purpose of all indicators, of course, is to get a clue to future price developments. If we could trade past prices we would all be millionaires. Indicators that have proven their effectiveness in the past have a great likelihood of working in the future as history has a tendency to repeat itself. But bear in mind that past results are no guarantee of future performance.

New indicators are continuously being invented. Some offer a genuinely new approach while others are only variations of classic indicators. Some analysts, such as Curtis Arnold, price pattern expert, believe that common indicators do not work any longer since everybody is using them. Most trading professionals I have spoken with, however, including John Bollinger, insist that indicators still work and that the basic ones like relative strength index, stochastics and moving averages work the best.

Rest assured that there is no single *magic indicator*, one that is capable of calling every turn of every market, every time. This creature does not, and will never, exist. Another common fallacy is to assume that by using five or more indicators together one can come up with a failsafe system. The problem with this approach is that the more indicators are used, the greater the likelihood that they will give conflicting signals. The secret of success is to find two or three indicators that work best with your trading style, time frame and markets you trade. A lot of chart studying and experimentation is necessary in the beginning. As with anything else in life, practice makes perfect.

The indicators introduced during the following pages may be all that you will ever need. They are representative for all basic indicator types: volatility, trend following, oscillating and trend measurement. It surely does no harm to have a powerful chart program like *MetaStock* with over 60 indicators, but it is best to first familiarize oneself, and fully understand, the basic indicators before venturing on to more exotic territory.

The ability to create custom indicators should be a feature to look for in a charting program for anybody interested in trading system development and testing.

Average True Range

The Average True Range indicator was made popular by Welles Wilder, Jr. by his book, *New Concepts in Technical Trading Systems*, (Greensboro, NC, Trend Research, 1978). In the book Wilder explains a trading system based on the indicator. The Average True Range is defined as follows. It is the greatest for each period:

- The distance from today's high to today's low.
- The distance from yesterday's close to today's high.
- The distance from yesterday's close to today's low.

Thus, the Average True Range is simply the average of the true ranges over the past x periods. The Average True Range is interpreted by using the same techniques that are used with the other volatility indicator such as standard deviation. Refer to the Standard Deviation paragraph for further information on volatility interpretation.

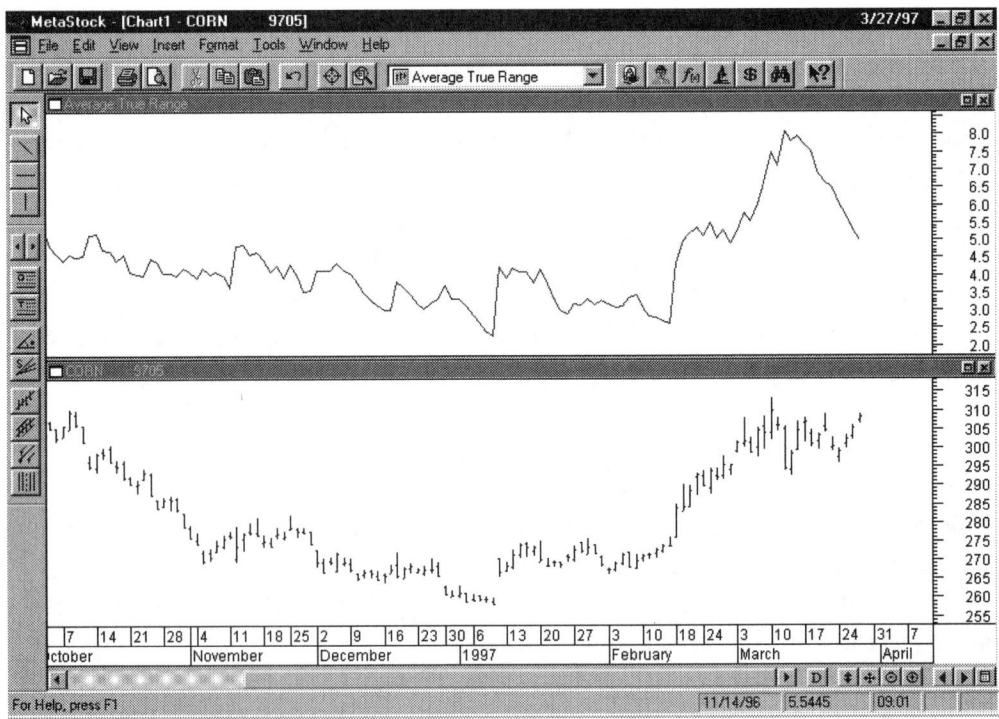

Figure 36. Bar chart of CBOT Corn with an Average True Range indicator plotted above (using a time period value of 5).

Bollinger Bands

Bollinger Bands are a combination moving average/envelope indicator developed by John Bollinger. Unlike standard envelopes, where the envelopes are plotted at a fixed percentage above and below the moving average, Bollinger Bands are plotted by using standard deviation levels.

Therefore the bands widen when the security becomes more volatile and contract when volatility decreases.

Bollinger Band interpretation:

- Sharp moves are likely to occur after the bands tighten, when volatility is low.
- Prices outside of the bands indicate a trend continuation.
- Trend reversals are likely when a top or bottom made outside the bands is followed by tops/bottoms made inside of the bands.
- A move that starts at one band often tends to go all the way to the other band. This observation is useful when projecting price targets.

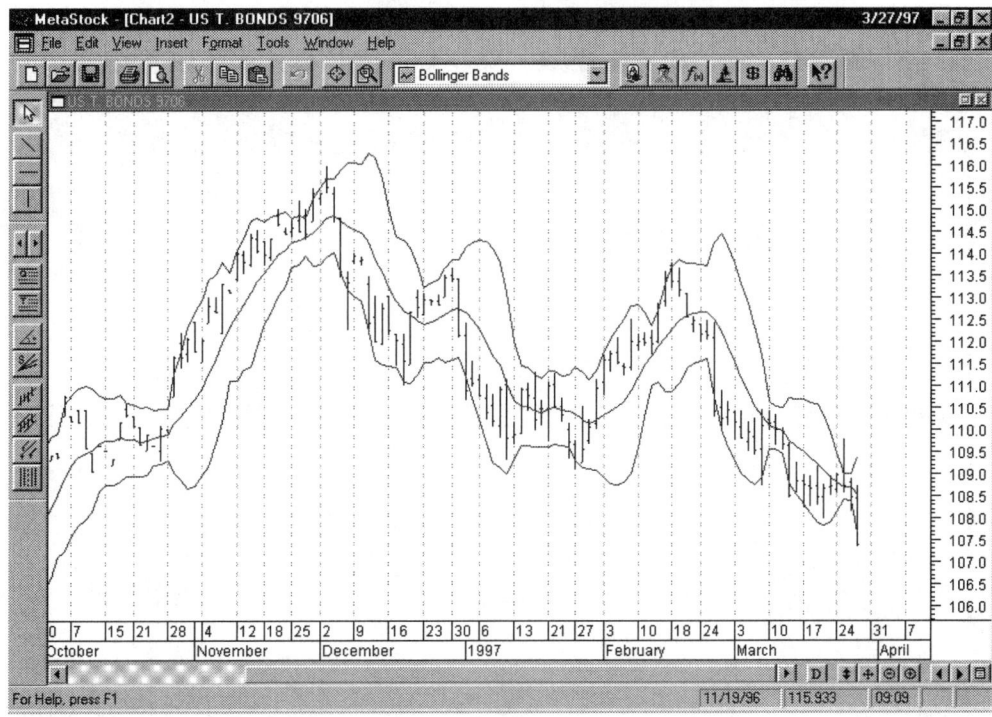

Figure 37. T-BOND bar chart with Bollinger Bands. Note how a reversal starting from one band often continues to to opposite side.

Directional Movement

Directional Movement was developed by Welles Wilder and is covered in detail in his book, *New Concepts in Technical Trading Systems*. The index actually consists of 4 components, +DI, -DI, ADX, and ADXR. What makes this indicator special is that ADX and ADXR can be used to measure the strength of trends. ADXR is a smoothed version of ADX. Because of this unique property directional movement has been incorporated into many mechanical trading systems.

The basic method of using the directional movement system is to plot the 14-period +DI and the 14-period -DI on top of each other. A buy signal is generated when +DI rises above -DI and a sell signal when +DI falls below -DI.

According to Wilder, these simple trading rules are filtered with the *extreme point rule*. This rule is designed to prevent whipsaws and reduce the number of trades. The extreme point rule requires that on the day that +DI and -DI cross the *extreme price* is noted. When long the extreme price is the low price on the day the lines cross. When short the extreme price is the high price on the day the lines cross.

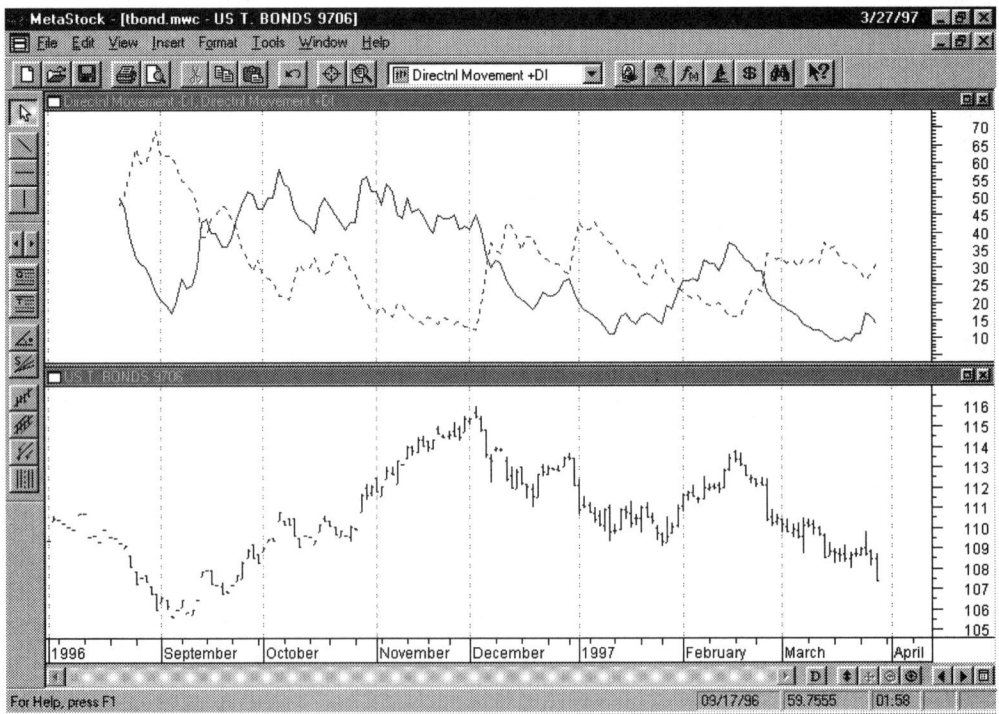

Figure 38. T-BOND bar chart with 14 day Directional Movement lines. +DI is the solid line and -DI the dotted line.

The extreme point is then used as a trigger point to initiate the trade. For example, when +DI rises above –DI the trader should wait until the security's price rises above the extreme point before buying. A failure of the price to rise above the extreme point would serve as a warning not to enter any new long positions and hold on to any existing short positions.

Wilder notes that his system works best on securities that have a high Commodity Selection Index (another indicator) value. "As a rule of thumb, the system will be profitable on commodities that have an ADXR value above 25. When the ADXR drops below 20, then do not use a trend-following system." What is often difficult for beginners to grasp is the fact that a rising ADX or ADXR indicate that prices are in a trending phase, regardless of market direction! Prices could be going up OR down.

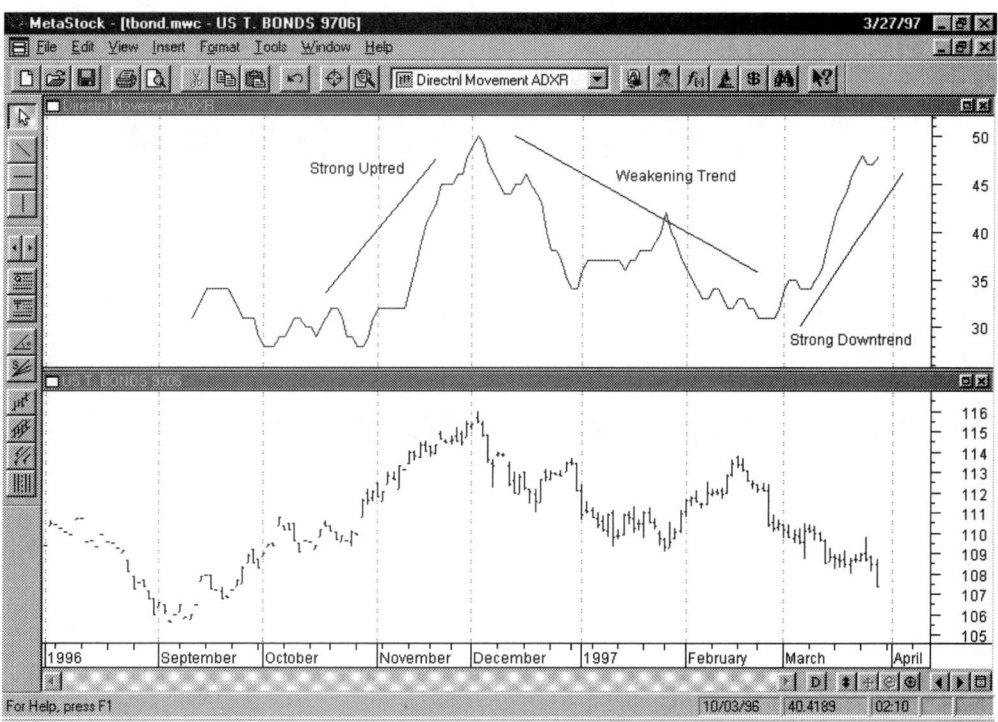

Figure 39. T-BOND bar chart with 10 day ADXR. A sharply rising ADXR signifies an increasing trend, which can be up or down.

MACD

MACD stands for Moving Average Convergence/Divergence. This popular indicator is calculated by subtracting a 0.075 (26-period) exponential moving average from a 0.15 (12-period) exponential moving average. A 9-period exponential moving average, called the *signal line*, is usually displayed as a dotted line on top of the MACD line.

The traditional MACD trading rule is to buy when the MACD rises above its 9-period signal line and sell when it falls below. As with other studies like RSI and Stochastics, MACD can be used to spot divergences (covered in detail later). These divergences often are more easily noticed when MACD is plotted as a histogram. A MACD histogram plots the difference between the MACD line and the signal line.

Figure 40. Amoco chart with MACD. Note the bearish divergence. Prices make a higher high, but on the MACD chart the second high is lower than the first. A bearish divergence warns of sudden price reversals. Even divergences are not fail-safe, however. Sometimes prices do not retreat until a second, or even third, bearish divergence.

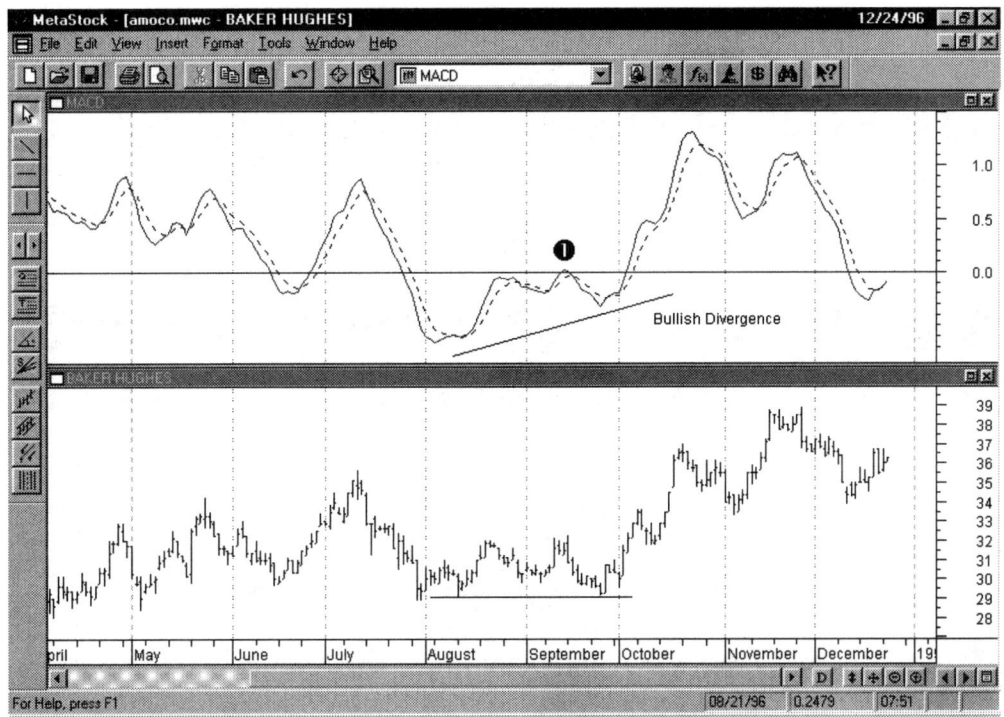

Figure 41. Chart of Baker Hughes with MACD. Note the bullish divergence. Prices made a low around the beginning of August and a second, equal, low towards the end of September. The corresponding low on the MACD chart was considerably higher however, creating a bullish divergence, calling for higher prices. Note point 1, which was also a part of a bullish divergence, but the rally didn't follow through — no indicator works each and every time.

Momentum / Rate of Change (ROC)

Momentum and ROC are basically the same as both indicators calculate rate-of-change. The difference is that ROC calculates the result as a percentage and Momentum as a ratio.

Momentum is a classic overbought/oversold oscillator indicator. When prices rise, so does the indicator. High Momentum values indicate an overbought market, low values an oversold market. If prices are going up and the momentum line is above 100 and rising, the uptrend is accelerating or gaining in strength. If the momentum line begins to flatten while prices are advancing the strength of the move is decreasing. The opposite is true in downtrends.

Example

To calculate a 12 day momentum simply subtract the closing price from 12 days ago from today's close. The result is either positive or negative, oscillating around a zero line. The actual formula is: Momentum = C-Cx. With C being the latest closing price and Cx being the close x days ago.

As with all overbought/oversold indicators, it is best to wait for the market to confirm a reversal before placing a trade, as a market may remain overbought/oversold for some time. Extremely overbought/oversold markets usually indicate continuation of a strong trend. A commonly used Momentum parameter is 10 days, which is suitable for short to intermediate-term analysis.

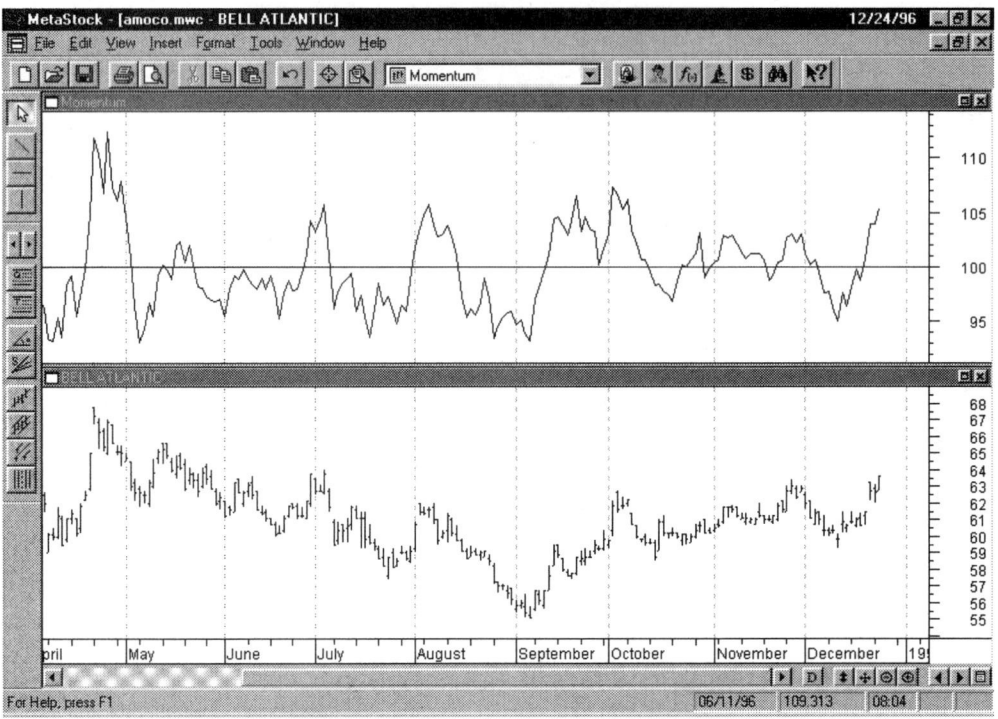

Figure 42. Chart of Bell Atlantic with a 10 day momentum. Price action during the time period chosen was pretty choppy, resulting in plenty of whipsaws on the momentum chart.

Moving Average

There is probably no better indicator for measuring trends than moving averages. Remember: *"The trend is your friend!"* The only problem with them is that they are *lagging* indicators, as they are trend followers. They do a great job of illustrating a market's direction when they are trending, but lag behind when sudden reversals occur. Thus they will generate good signals in strong trending markets, but will whipsaw when prices are in a trading range.

Example

A moving average is calculated the following way: add the closing price for a number of time periods (for example, the last 14 days) and then divide the sum by the amount of periods used. The result is the average price for today. Each day this calculation is repeated and the result plotted on a chart. By connecting these points a line is formed, which is the moving average.

Figure 41. Chart of Brystol Myers with a 20 day moving average. In a trending market like this one moving averages work very well.

Figure 42. Chart of Burlington Northern with a 20 day moving average. Trading a choppy market like this one with a moving average would result in several losses.

The basic way to trade a moving average is extremely simple: buy when prices close above the moving average, sell when prices close below the moving average. As the number of periods used to calculate a moving average is variable, here are some commonly used values:

5-13 Periods	**Very Short Term Trend**
14-24 Periods	**Short Term Trend**
25-50 Periods	**Intermediate Trends**
51-100 Periods	**Longer Term Trends**
101-200+ Periods	**Long Term Trends**

Better trading signals are usually obtained by using two moving averages instead of one. A buy signal is generated when the shorter (more sensitive) one crosses above the longer one. A sell signal occurs when the shorter one crosses below the longer one. Commonly used moving average combinations are : 5 & 10, 9 & 18, 50 & 200.

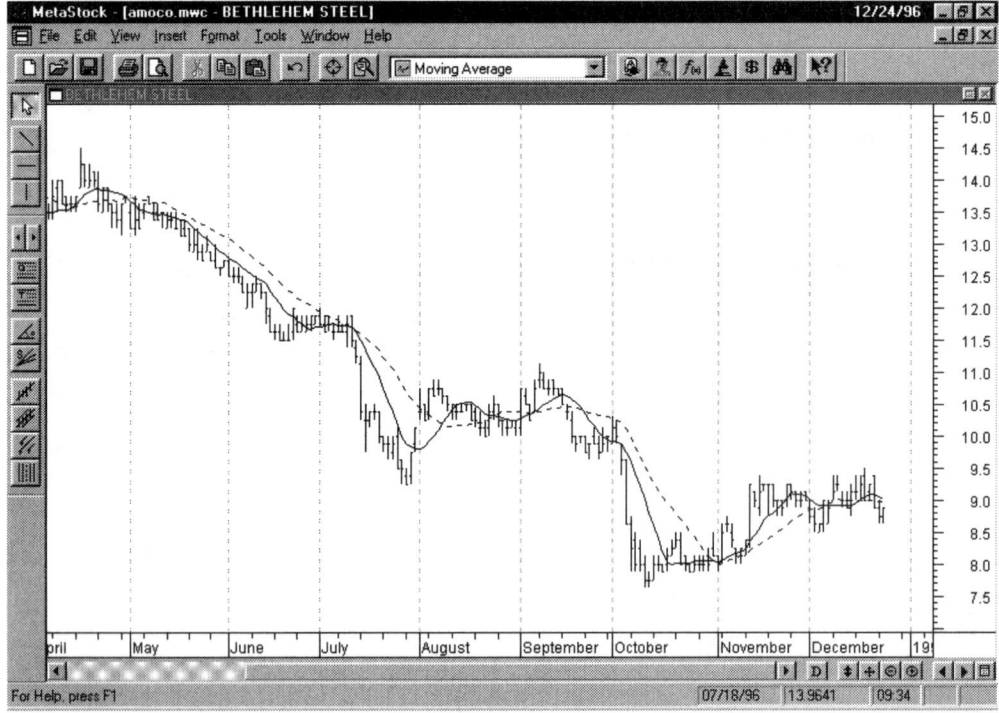

Figure 43. Chart of Bethlehem Steel with 10 day (solid line) and 20 day (dotted line) moving averages. A long position is entered when the solid line crosses above the dotted line, and a short position is entered when the solid line crosses below the dotted line.

On Balance Volume (OBV)

This indicator, developed by Joseph Granville (*New Strategy of Daily Stock Market Timing for Maximum Profit,* Prentice-Hall. 1976), shows volume flowing in and out of a security. It is used as a short term leading indicator. OBV is calculated as follows:

- If today's close is larger than yesterday's close then OBV = yesterday's OBV plus today's volume.

- If today's close is smaller than yesterday's close then OBV = yesterday's OBV minus today's volume.

- If today's close is equal to yesterday's close then OBV = yesterday's OBV

For intraday trading the OBV formula is modified to work with tick size. If the last tick was up then OBV = Last OBV plus tick size. If the last tick was down then OBV = last OBV minus tick size.

Figure 44. Chart of Avon Products with OBV. Note how major peaks on the OBV coincide with tops on the price chart.

Parabolic SAR

This study got its name because the dotted lines this indicator uses resemble a parabola. In a way it's a miniature trading system. SAR stands for Stop and Reverse, which means that this indicator is always in the market, either short or long. When the dots are under the price bars the indicator is long, and the dots represent the stop-loss level. When the dots are above the price bars the system is short, and again, the dot is the stop-loss level. Note that Parabolic starts out by giving a trade plenty of room, but tightens stops considerably at later stages.

Figure 44. Chart of American Express with a standard Parabolic SAR. Note how the Parabolic indicator is always in the market, being either long or short. Also note that the stop-loss levels are not necessarily appropriate for one's personal trading style.

Standard Deviation

Standard Deviation is a statistical measurement of volatility. Standard Deviation is typically used as a component of an indicator, rather than as a standalone indicator. For example, Bollinger Bands are calculated by adding the standard deviation to a moving average. High Standard Deviation values signify high volatility. Prices are deviating from their moving average significantly. Low standard deviation values signify low volatility, prices are remaining close to their moving average.

Typically, low Standard Deviation values (i.e., low volatility) tend to come before significant breakouts. Many analysts believe that major tops are normally accompanied with high volatility, and major bottoms by low volatility.

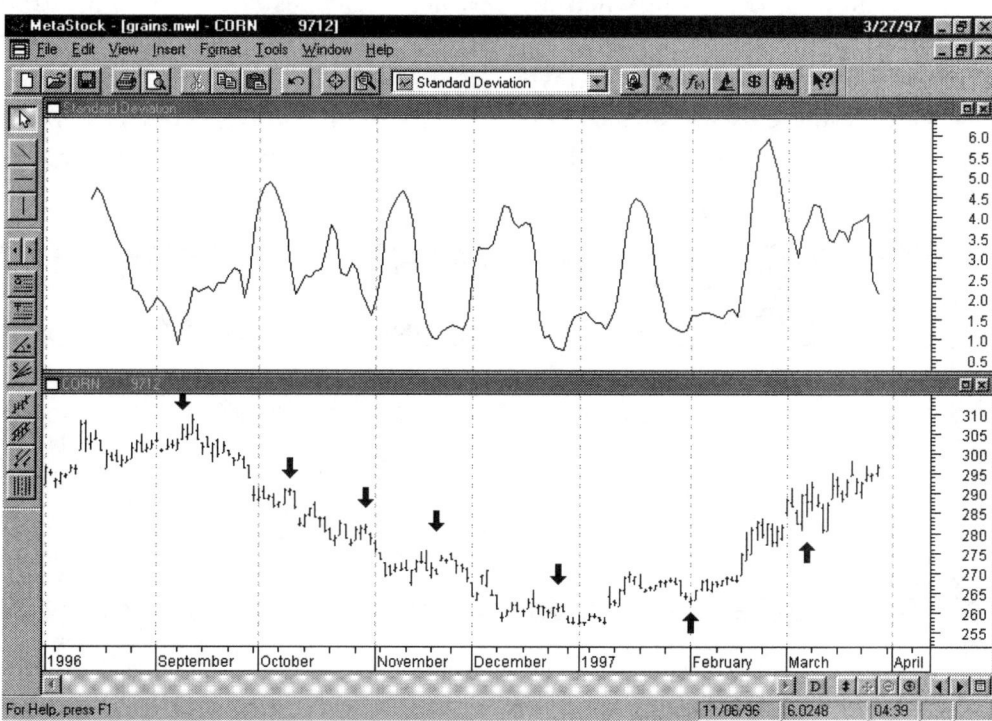

Figure 45. Chart of CBOT Corn and a 10 day Standard Deviation. Note how periods of low standard deviation offer good entry points within the prevailing trend.

Stochastics

This study, developed by George Lane, is based on the observation that as prices rise, closing prices tend to be closer to the upper end of the trading range. In a downtrend the closing price would be near the lower end of the trading range. The purpose of the study is to determine where the recent closing price is in relation to the price range for a given time period. The most commonly used time frame is 5. The study consists of two lines, the %K and the %D. The %D is a 3 day moving average of the %K line. %K is plotted as a solid line, while the %D is plotted as a dashed line. Stochastics has a value ranging from 0 to 100. A high reading (over 70) means that closing prices are near the top of the range (an overbought condition), a low reading (under 30) that prices are close to the bottom of the range (an oversold condition). Keep in mind that markets can stay overbought and oversold for quite some time when a strong trend is under way. A trading signal to go long is present when the %K and %D lines cross above 30 from below. Go short when the %K and %D lines go below 70 from above. Especially good trading signals are generated when divergences between price and the %D line precede the crossing of the 30 or 70 marker. Stochastics work best when markets are in a trading range and may give false signals when a strong trend is under way.

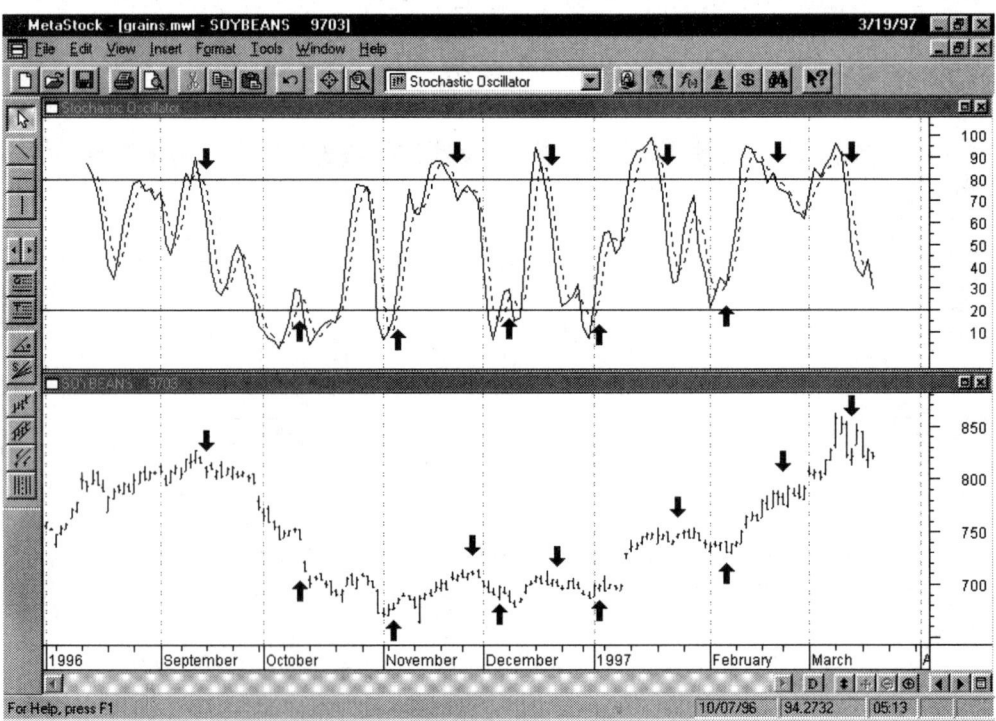

Figure 46. Chart of CBOT Soybeans with Stochastics. Note how the standard Stochastic trading approach can generate bad signals when a market is trending, like September/October and January through March.

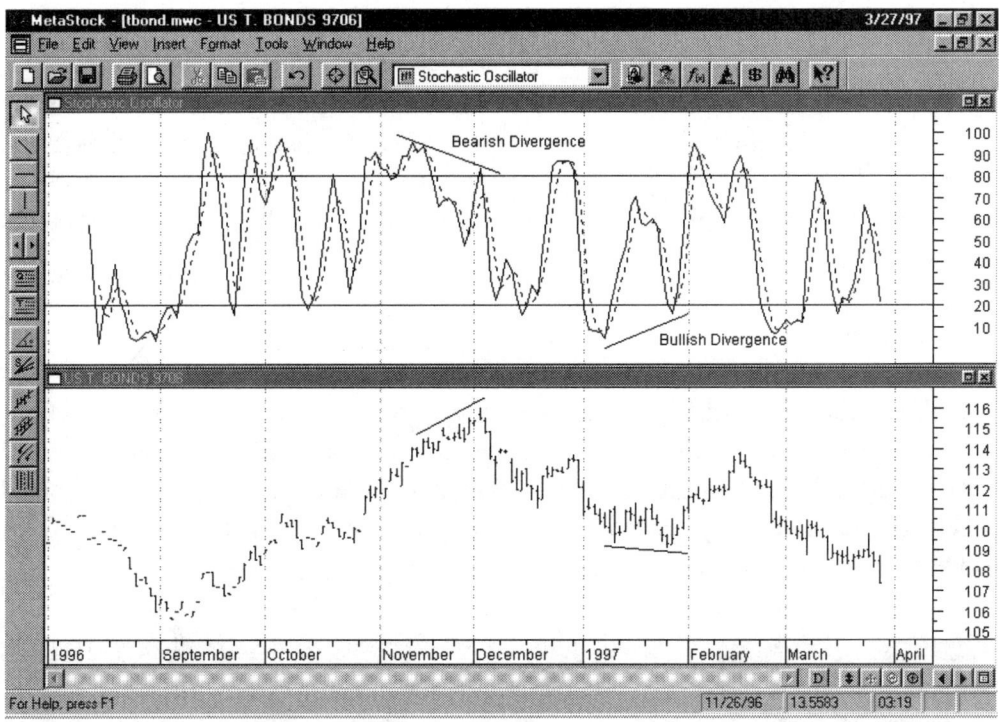

Figure 47. T-Bond chart and Stochastics. Bearish divergences above the 70 marker and bullish divergences below the 30 marker warn very reliably of reversals.

Line Studies

These seemingly simple technical analysis techniques should not be underestimated as they often prove to be just as effective as many complex indicators. Another advantage is that a pencil and ruler is all that is needed (besides the chart, of course), making trendlines and the like the technique of choice when computers are not available.

Trendlines

The following chart illustrates that even simple trendlines can provide effective ways to evaluate a market. Trendlines that are touched 3 or more times are considered to be more significant than lines that are touched only twice. Support refers to lines that "support" prices from heading lower while resistance signifies price levels that are difficult to exceed to the upside.

Figure 48. Corn chart and various trendlines. To the left a trend "channel" is visible. Prices are deemed to be in a price channel when they oscillate between (parallel) support and resistance lines. Also note how support often turns into resistance lines.

Figure 49 & 50. Weekly charts of American Electric and DTE Energy. Trendlines can also be drawn using the close instead of highs and lows (a matter of preference). Note the bullish setup on this chart as prices dipped below the support line, rebounded, and took out the previous February high. Note the bearish setup during March of 1996. Prices violated the upside trendline and then failed to stay above the October 1995 high.

Fibonacci Retracements

Leonardo Fibonacci was an Italian mathematician around the year 1170. It is said that Fibonacci discovered the relationship of what are now called Fibonacci numbers while studying the Great Pyramid of Giza in Egypt.

Retracements are based on the fact that after an initial move prices often give back, or retrace, a part of their gains (or losses in case of a down move). Interestingly, these countermoves often stop at certain, predictable percentages. Fibonacci Retracements are based on the following percentages: 38.2%, 50% and 61.8%. There are quite a few books on the market that deal extensively with Fibonacci numbers and retracements. Please refer to such publications such as *Understanding Fibonacci Numbers* and *Fibonacci Ratios with Pattern Recognition* available through Traders Press for details on the subject.

Figure 51. Daily chart of DTE Energy. Fibonacci retracements were calculated using the move from point 1 to point 2. Note how prices stopped at Fibonacci levels at points 4 &5, but didn't seem to take notice at point 3. Retracements are best used together with other indicators and studies.

Gann Lines

W. D. Gann's (1878-1955) life and trading techniques are shrouded in mystery, rumor and hearsay. He supposedly died having amassed a 50 million dollar fortune trading, but according to other sources he only left a house and $150,000 behind.

Central to Gann's technique is the use of geometric angles combining time and price. Gann believed that specific geometric patterns and angles had unique characteristics that could be used to predict price action. All of Gann's techniques require that equal time and price intervals be used on the charts, so that 1x1 line will equal a 45 degree angle.

Gann believed that the ideal balance between time and price exists when prices rise or fall at a 45 degree angle relative to the time axis, also called a 1x1 angle. Gann angles are drawn between significant bottoms and tops (or vice versa) at various angles. The most important, according to Gann, is the 1x1 trendline. It signifies a bull market when prices are above the trendline and bear market when below. Gann felt that the 1x1 trendline provides major support during an uptrend. When the trendline is broken a major reversal is in progress.

Gann Angles

1 x 8	-	82.5 degrees
1 x 4	-	75 degrees
1 x 3	-	71.25 degrees
1 x 2	-	63.75 degrees
1 x 1	-	45 degrees
2 x 1	-	26.25 degrees
3 x 1	-	18.75 degrees
4 x 1	-	15 degrees
8 x 1	-	7.5 degrees

In order for prices to match the actual angles the x- and y-axes must have equally spaced intervals. This means that one unit on the x-axis (hour, day, week) must be the same distance as one unit on the y-axis. The easiest way to calibrate the chart is make sure that a 1x1 angle produces a 45 degree angle.

Gann noticed that each angle can provide support and resistance depending on the trend. In addition to Gann Lines, Gann also developed several other techniques for studying market action which include Gann Fans and Gann Grids.

Example

During an uptrend the 1 x 1 angle tends to provide major support. A major reversal is signaled when prices fall below this line. Then prices should fall to the next trendline (the 2 x 1 angle). In other words, as one angle is penetrated, expect prices to move and consolidate at the next angle.

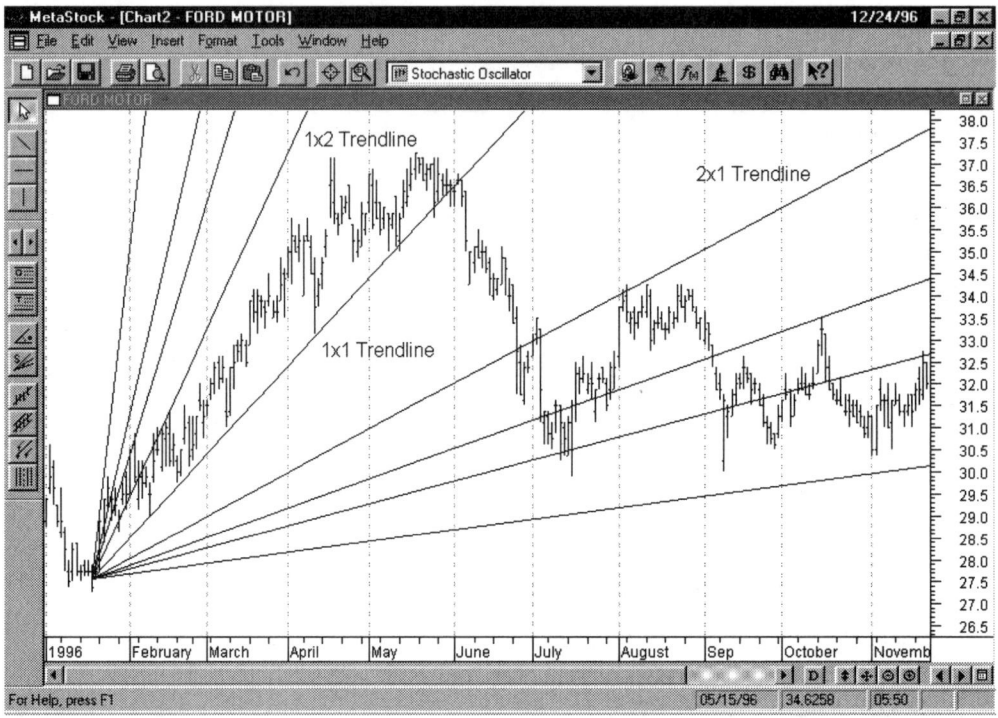

Figure 52. Daily chart of Ford and Gann Lines. See how the 1x1 trendline provided support throughout the bull move. When prices penetrated the trendline in June, support and resistance were supplied by other Gann Lines.

Chart Formations and Patterns

Using chart formations and patterns as a means to predict future price movement is based on the premise that history tends to repeat itself. Certain past events often lead to predictable future events. To a certain degree the use of patterns to find trading opportunities has become a self-fulfilling prophecy; by how much is up to debate. Remember, there are thousands of people like you out there who are all looking at the exact same charts, knowing exactly what they mean. Yet, interpreting formations and patterns is somewhat of an art, as there is plenty of room for subjectivity. What is an obvious triangle or wedge for one trader may be of no significance to another. Experienced traders often enter a trade early by anticipating the likely effect of a pattern. This way they hope to get a "head start" on a move. This approach has some merit but should be used only by traders that have several years of chart reading experience. Patterns fall into two categories: reversal and continuation patterns. Reversal patterns include head and shoulders, inverted head and shoulders, double top and bottom and triple top and bottom. A reversal pattern obviously warns of a change in trend. A continuation pattern, on the other hand, signifies a period of consolidation, after which the prevailing trend continues. Triangles, which can come in many shapes and sizes, and flags are basic continuation patterns.

Some traders also refer to patterns as the combination of several bars (usually between 3 and 6), similar in principle to candlestick analysis. In fact, there is specialized software on the market, NAVA Patterns being one, that automatically identifies patterns that have been statistically proven to have high forecasting value. Finding and testing patterns can be quite involving and is beyond the scope of this book.

Head and Shoulders

This reversal formation comes in a top and bottom variety. With the topping formation one can notice a peak, the head, surrounded by two lower highs, the shoulders, which are more or less equal in height. By connecting the valleys of the lower peaks with a line one gets the "neckline." By measuring the distance from the neckline to the head and projecting the same distance from the neckline down one can estimate how far a move will go. The bottom head and shoulder formation is simply a mirror image of the one just discussed. The implication in this case is, of course, bullish instead of bearish. The examples used on the next page are deliberately not perfect textbook examples to illustrate a variety of possible head and shoulder scenarios. To avoid trading a head and shoulders pattern too early many analysts recommend to enter the trade only after two consecutive closes below/above the neckline.

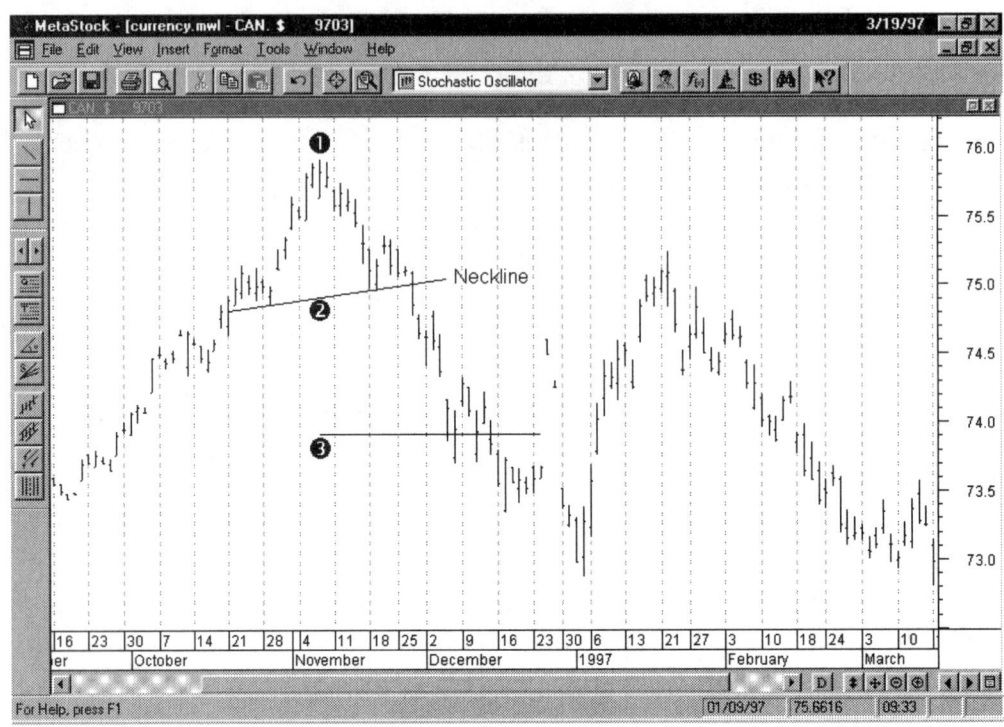

Figure 53. Daily chart of March 97 Canadian $. The shoulders in this example are quite small. Note how prices briefly paused in the price target area before receding further.

Figure 54. Daily chart of American Electric Power. A failed bottom head and shoulder. Notice how prices failed to penetrate the neckline after the right shoulder at point 1. After making a third "shoulder" prices broke the neckline, but didn't reach the price target area.

Figure 55. Daily chart of DTE Energy. Notice how prices bounced off the price target area before continuing to fall.

Double & Triple Tops and Bottoms

Figure 56 & 57. Daily chart of Homestake Mining. Note the high made in February. This high should not be used to make a triple top as it happened too far in the past. However, prices almost made a triple top around the first of June before retreating. The Chrysler chart below illustrates a classic double bottom formation.

Figure 58. Daily chart of American General. Notice how the triple top leads to a double bottom.

Triangles

As mentioned earlier, triangles are continuation patterns and may also be called wedges or pennants, depending on their size. A trend that may have been getting ahead of itself is going through a period of consolidation. Therefore, a breakout of a triangle in an uptrend will generally be to the upside, while a breakout of a triangle in a downtrend will most likely lead to lower prices. Note that trading volume should increase with the breakout.

The three basic triangle shapes are the ascending, descending and symmetrical triangle. The ascending triangle is easily spotted as prices keep stopping at the same level to the upside while the respective lows keep getting higher. The breakout to the upside can be expected in the last third of the triangle. A descending triangle has highs that are steadily decreasing while the lows are stopping at the same level. The breakout to the downside usually happens in the last third of the triangle. Every so often a *false breakout* will occur, which means that prices will break out shortly to the wrong side, only to reverse and then head to the anticipated direction.

Figure 59. Daily chart of June 1997 Eurodollar. Breakout to the upside confirmed continuation of the uptrend. Of course, there is no way to know how long a continuation will last.

Figure 60. Daily chart of McDonalds. Symmetrical triangles have the tendency to break out in either direction.

Figure 61. Daily chart of Polaroid. The descending triangle 1 behaved as expected. Triangle 2, however, did not result in a further downturn. Triangles that continue to the end of the angle often demonstrate this behavior.

Note

Finding and defining triangles is extremely subjective, much more so than head and shoulder and double top and bottom formations. Some analysts include price action going back several months (on a daily chart), while others only take the last month or so into consideration. In my personal judgement the former gives better long term signals while the latter approach seems to work best for short term trading.

Flags

Flags are among the most reliable continuation patterns. A bullish flag should be preceded by a sharp move to the upside, while it slopes against the trend. Volume should diminish during this period of consolidation. A break of the flag's resistance line (the top line) should be confirmed by an increase in volume. A bearish flag appears within a downtrend and slopes upward against the trend. A trade is entered when the bottom support line has been decisively penetrated.

Figure 62. Daily chart of Merrill Lynch. The arrows indicate where to go long.

Figure 63. Daily chart of CME Japanese Yen. The arrow indicates where to go short.

Case Study 1: A Simple Moving Average System

Before we proceed with our first actual trading system I would like present the following three charts. Could be anything, correct? A stock, commodity or currency. One can identify formations, like the ones covered earlier and draw some meaningful trendlines. There are even a few nice trends and trading ranges.

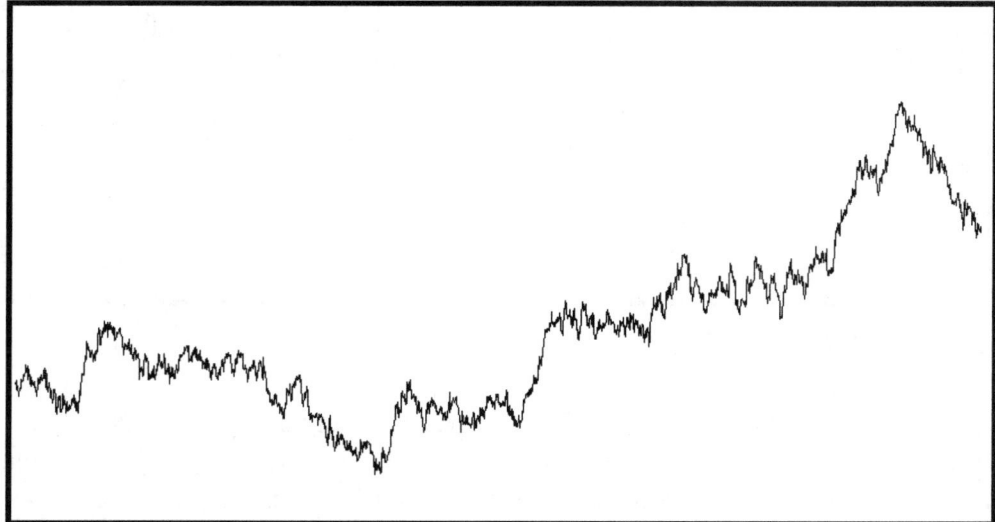

Figure 64. Mystery chart 1.

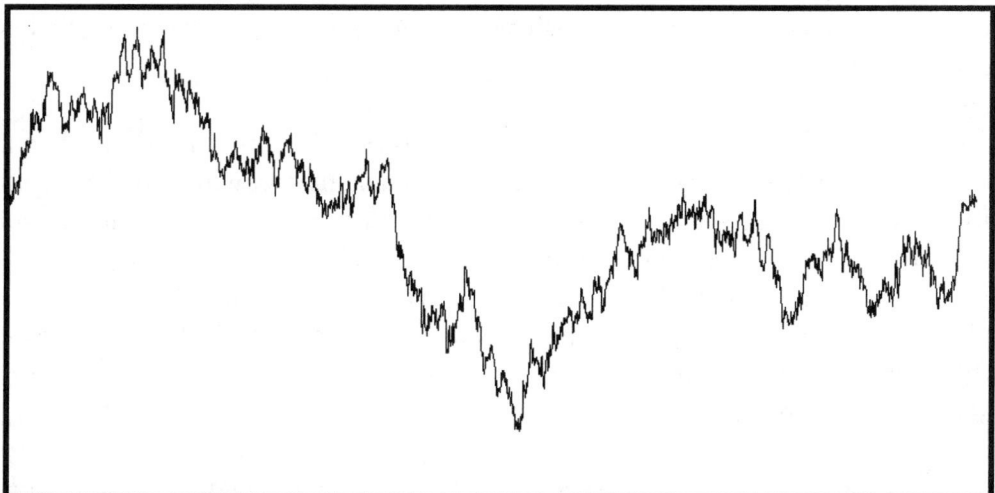

Figure 65. Mystery chart 2.

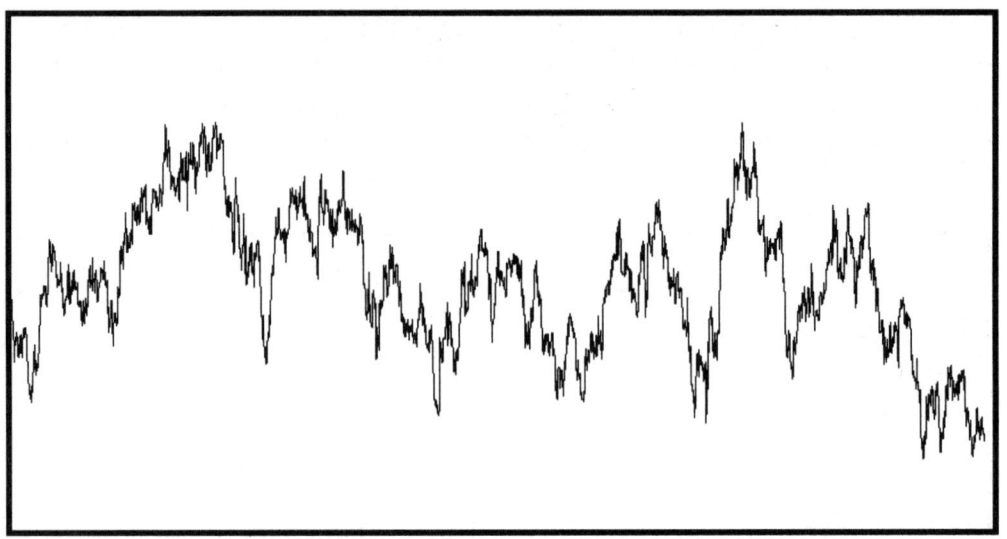

Figure 66. Mystery chart 3.

The amazing truth is that all 3 charts are not from any actual security at all, but were created with an Excel random number macro provided courtesy of *Rabatin Investment Research*. Without getting too much into the mathematical details involved, this macro generates pseudo-random charts. If a day closes up or down is totally random, only the amount of the move is based to a certain degree on the previous "day." These charts have stunned quite a few market professionals, believe me! If actual market charts look no different than the ones this small program can create, then this leads to the conclusion that all markets must buy random to a certain degree as well.

Which leads to another interesting conclusion: Nobody can know when a trend will start or stop, and nobody knows where any market will be X days from today! Yet, with a decent trading system and proper money management one can make money! This revelation of course implies that all forecasts made by "market gurus" and analysts are nothing more than pure guesses. Which once again proves the point to stick to ones own trading system, whatever it may be based on, since the other guys cannot, and do not have, a crystal ball to see the future. Pretty heady stuff. And you are free to disagree.

For those interested in market theory I would recommend *A Random Walk Down Wall Street: Including a Life-Cycle Guide to Personal Investing* by Burton Malkiel and "Chaos and Order in the Capital Markets: A New View of Prices, Cycles and Market Volatility" by Egar Peters. The latter book covers rather esoteric subjects like random walk and efficient markets, fractal statistics and fractals and chaos.

So far we have looked at chart types, indicators, studies and trading fundamentals. Now it is time to put it all together and see if we can come up with an actual trading system. Don't expect this one to be a real moneymaker however. The purpose of our first system is only to illustrate the steps involved and issues that need to be addressed.

Almost all successful system traders are trend followers. This means that their system is based on catching a developing trend and staying with it as long as possible. The intention is not so much to make a profit on each and every trade (would be nice), but to participate on those long, powerful moves that most markets have several times a year. The hefty profits that these trades generate are needed to compensate for the inevitable frequent small losses. Once again, this is why money management and loss control are so important: a big winner can make up for several *small* losers, and leave some profits left over, but not for several *large* losers.

The best basic indicator for designing trend following systems is a moving average. Moving averages (MA) can be simple, exponential or weighted. Weighted and exponential MA's give more importance, or weight, to recent price action than a simple MA. A weighted moving average is calculated by multiplying each of the previous day's data by a weight. An exponential moving average is calculated by applying a percentage of today's closing price to yesterday's moving average value.

Note

Interestingly, extensive testing by system developers and authors Charles LeBeau and David Lucas (*Computer Analysis of the Futures Market*) has shown that trading systems using exponential and weighted MA's do not show better results than the ones using simple MA's.

We will begin designing our system by choosing a market that shows both phases markets can be in, sideways and trending. If one were to select a stock or commodity, which went straight up or down, a trend following indicator would obviously show fantastic results. This would not be very realistic, however. Secondly, one needs to decide upon the time parameter to use. A 3-day MA is very short term and a 200-day MA would be too long a time frame for most traders. I have found that a 10-day MA is a good all-around number to use. Ten trading days are two calendar weeks, not too long and not too short. Top analyst Walter Bressert believes that many commodity markets (gold, S&P) have 20-day and 20-week cycles (using weekly charts), so that 10 days would represent a half-cycle.

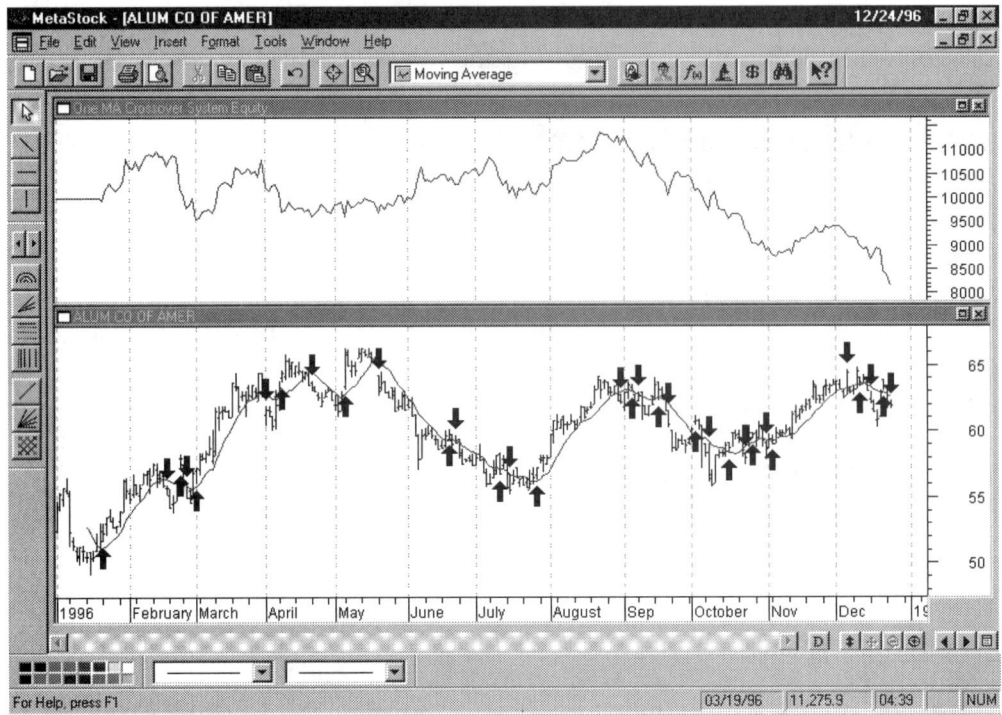

Figure 67. Chart of Aluminum Corporation of America with a 10-day MA. Arrows denote where the system goes long and short. Top chart is the equity curve based on a $10,000 investment.

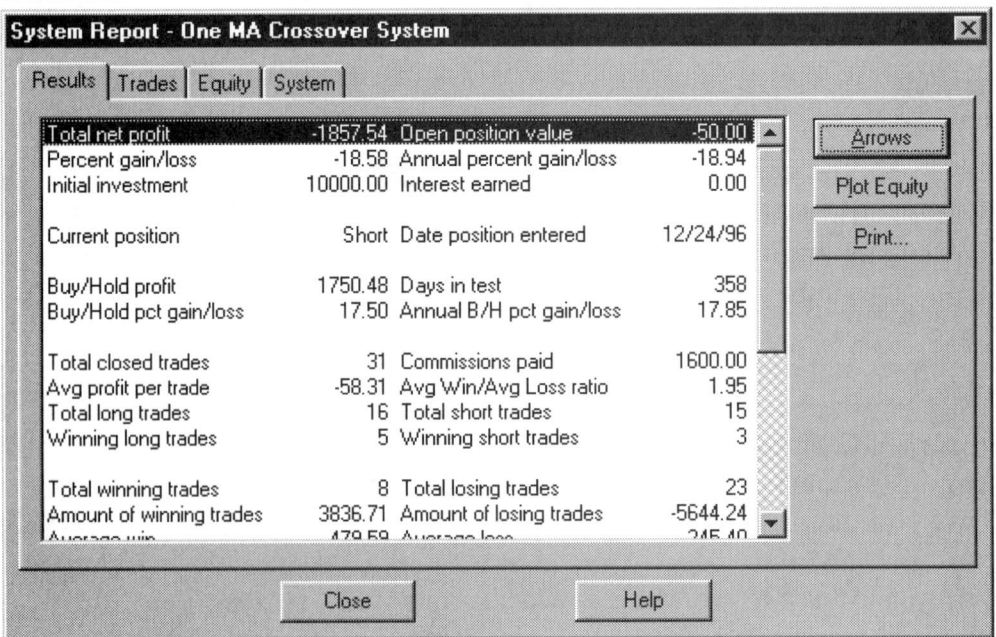

Figure 68. Performance report of the single MA crossover system.

Whipsaws Galore

Figure 68 shows a chart of Aluminum Co. of America with a simple 10-day MA. This system goes long (up arrow) when prices close above the MA and goes short (down arrow) when prices close below. This system enters the trade at the open, the day after the signal is generated which is the most realistic scenario. An initial investment of $10,000 and $50 commission for each complete trade (buying and selling) are assumed.

The top graph illustrates the system's equity curve. As you can see, the system did OK until September when choppy price action caused *whipsaws* (getting stopped in and out of trades). At the end of the period observed the system wound up losing roughly $1,900. It simply traded too often, with $50 (the minimum to figure for slippage and commission) going to the broker each time, for a total of $1,600! Figure 69 shows a part of the trade report.

Reducing the amount of trades should obviously improve the system's profitability. But instead of simply increasing the MA parameter to 15 days or longer, we will add a second MA. One with a longer time frame, for instance 20 days. Now we will trade the crossing of the MA lines themselves and not the crossing of the MA line and price bars.

Figure 69. Trading system using a dual MA (10 & 20) crossover system. Note how the system trades less frequently than before.

What we are doing is using two different, smoothed, versions of price action. One shorter term, the 10-day MA, and a somewhat longer time frame, the 20-day MA. By trading the crossing of these two indicators we are reducing the risk of being stopped out prematurely due to market *noise*. This term refers to price activity that is of no real importance, kind of like background static with AM radio. Figure 69 shows that our new approach significantly reduced the amount of trades.

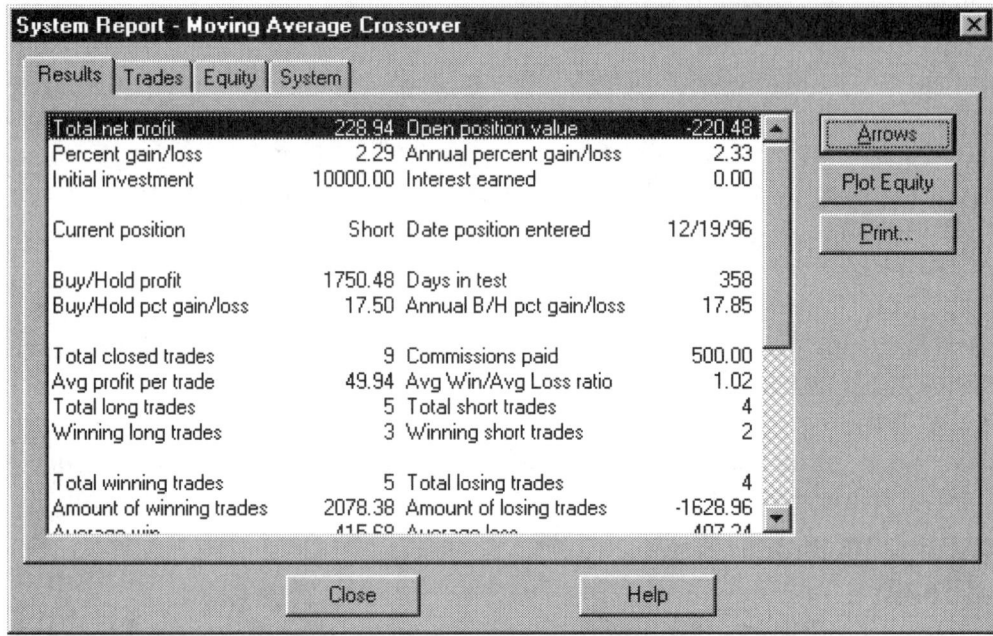

Figure 70. Performance report of the dual MA crossover system. Note how the amount of commission paid has been reduced to $500 because the system trades much less.

The dual MA system even generates a small profit, $228, compared to a nasty $1900 loss with the single 10 MA approach. Not only have we reduced the amount of trades, and thus commission and slippage, but we have also avoided being stopped in and out of several uninteresting trades. Let me stress an important point one more time: *Overtrading is deadly!*

Can this system be enhanced further? Yes! Without even getting into more sophisticated entry and exit techniques, if one had only taken the long trades instead of both long and short, the end results would look like the report in Figure 71. According to Nelson Freeburg, Director of *Formula Research*, a company that evaluates trading systems, 70% of a major stock's price action is directly correlated to the over all index activity (S&P 500), 20% to the industry group and only 10% to the stock itself. Therefore, if both the index and industry group are trending up, only long trades should be considered.

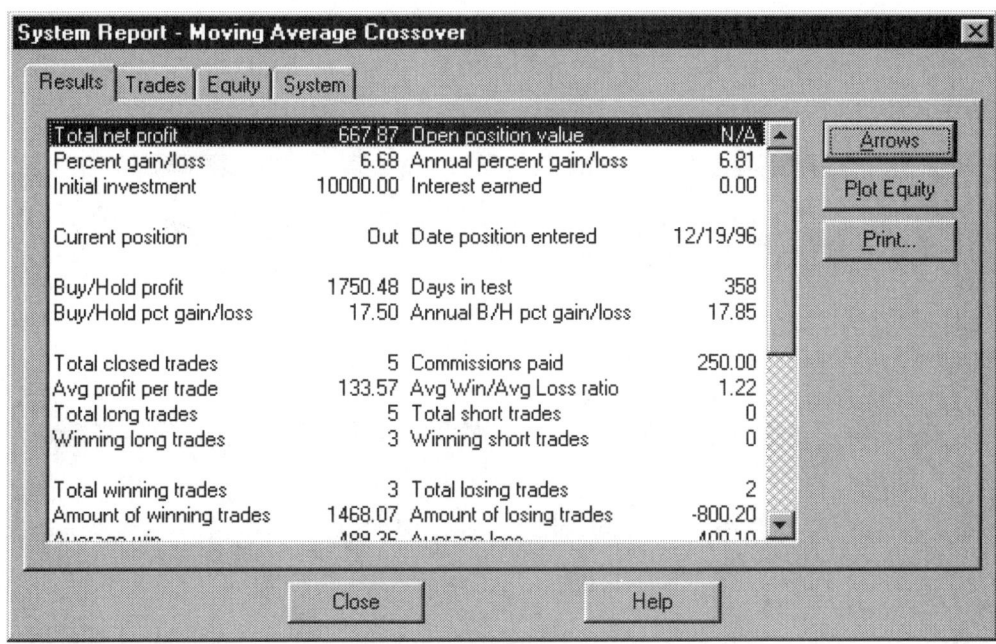

Figure 71. Performance report of the dual MA crossover system taking only long trades.

The dangers of parameter optimization

Most of the better charting packages on the market support a so-called *optimization* feature. What this lets one do is give an indicator a range of numbers to see which one generates the most profit.

Example

Instead of just assigning the values 10 and 20 to our MA's, the computer is told to try out all combinations within certain ranges, line 3-20 for MA1 and 10-30 for MA2. The larger the ranges are, the longer it will take the computer to finish the job. After each run the system notes how much profits were generated, ranking them when testing has been completed.

Figures 72 and 73 on the next page illustrate the amazing improvement to our dual MA crossover system. The optimal values turned out to be 10 for MA1 and 14 for MA2. Is optimizing the way to go to generate sure profits? Unfortunately, the answer is NO! All we really have succeeded in doing is curve fitting. We found out which parameters would have worked best in the PAST, and as all disclaimers (you know, the fine print) state, past performance is no guarantee of future results. Some analysts believe that a certain degree of optimization is tolerable since each market has its own characteristics and cycles, and that everything in life is optimized. One is attracted to specific types of the opposite sex, reads certain books and so forth. Other analysts think that a given system (with fixed parameters) must work with all, or most, markets to be acceptable. As always, the truth is somewhere in between.

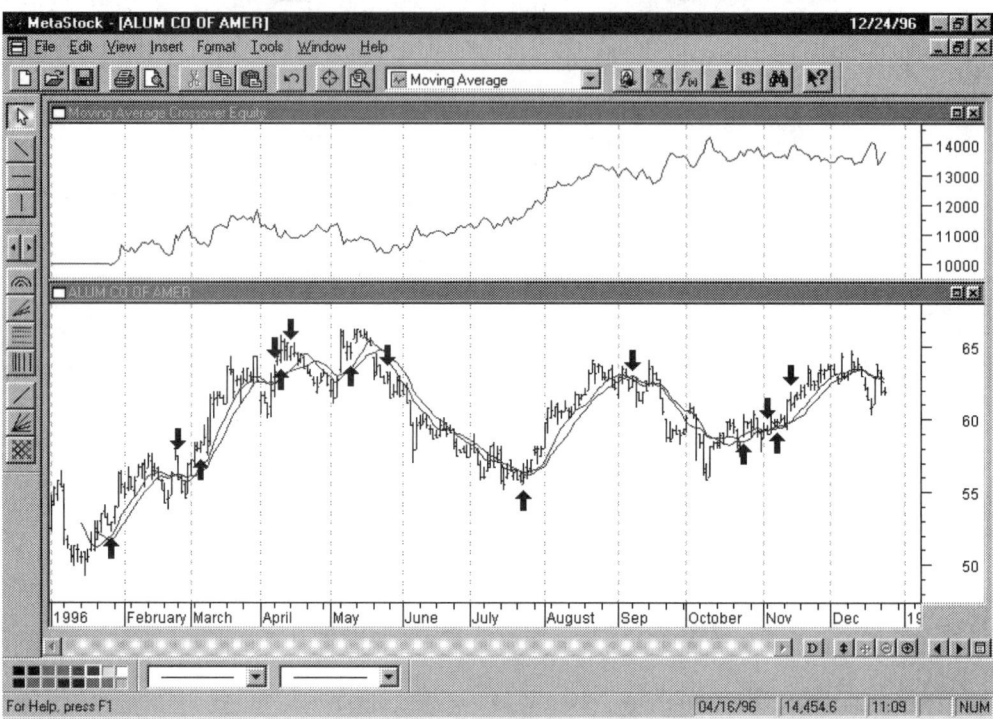

Figure 72. The dual MA crossover system with optimized parameters (10 & 14).

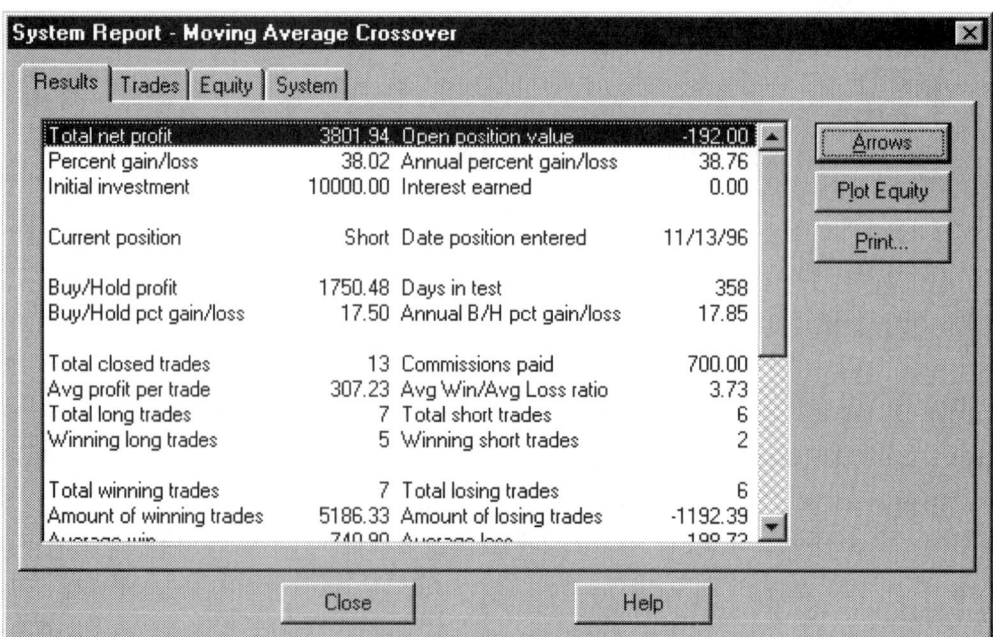

Figure 73. The system report now shows a net profit of almost $4,000.

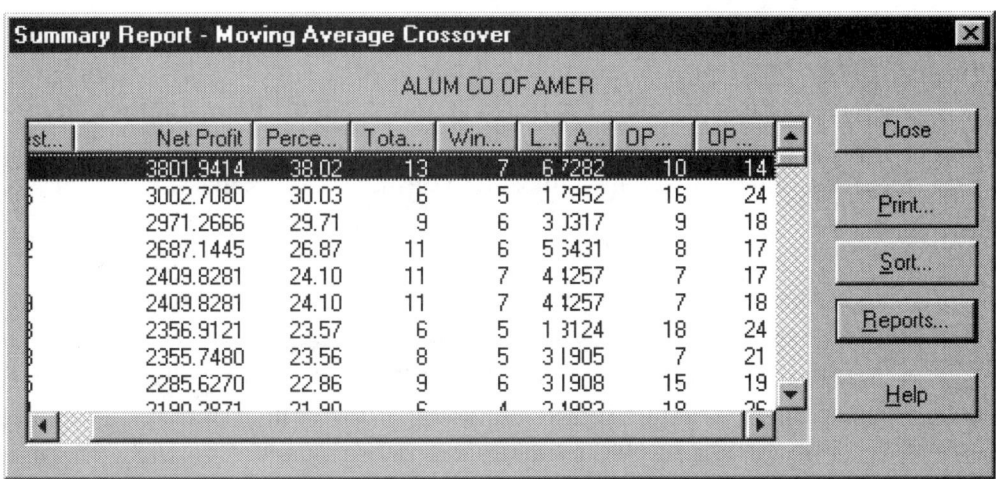

Figure 74. This part of the system report shows which MA combinations (the two right OP columns) generated the most profits.

Figure 73 shows which MA combinations resulted in the highest profits. Note that the top 3 had the following MA pairs: 10 & 14, 16 & 24, 9 & 18. The fact that these pairs vary so much is a dead giveaway that the top combinations were only so good because of over-optimization. In order for one to consider optimized parameters at all, one must make sure that the nearby combinations performed similarly well. Looking down the list of Figure 73 one notices that the 7/17, 7/18, 8/17 all did reasonably well. A day more or less did not drastically alter performance. If these parameters work equally well on this stock's price history which is out of sample (previous or later prices that were not used during the optimization process), one might be on to something!

Case Study 2: A Classic Breakout System

Range & volatility breakouts

While the dual crossover system kicks in with some delay after a trend has already begun, a breakout system enters a trade the day after the "breakout," giving the trader a head start should the move continue. As the name implies, prices are breaking out of their previous boundary. When this happens it is probable that some kind of fundamental change will lead to further action in the direction of the breakout.

The two basic types are the *range breakout* and the *volatility breakout*. The range breakout is characterized by a long, narrow trading range (the longer the better, at least 15 days) from which prices suddenly break decisively. On the day of the breakout, the close must be significantly higher/lower than during the trading range. A volatility breakout, on the other hand, doesn't require the presence of a trading range. Prices only need to close higher, or lower, than the highest high or lowest low during the last X days, where X can be 10, 20 or more. I personally prefer range breakouts since they can be spotted by simply eyeballing charts. In addition, a breakout from a long trading range seems to have more consistent follow-through. With both approaches you will experience the inevitable false breakout, where prices break out for a day or two, only to reverse and go in the opposite direction. These can represent interesting trading opportunities in themselves.

Figure 75. Range breakout (and volatility breakout at the same time). The bar with the arrow closes higher than any bar during the last 30 days.

Figure 76. Volatility breakouts. The arrows show the day on which prices closed higher/lower than the highest high or lowest low during the last 20 days.

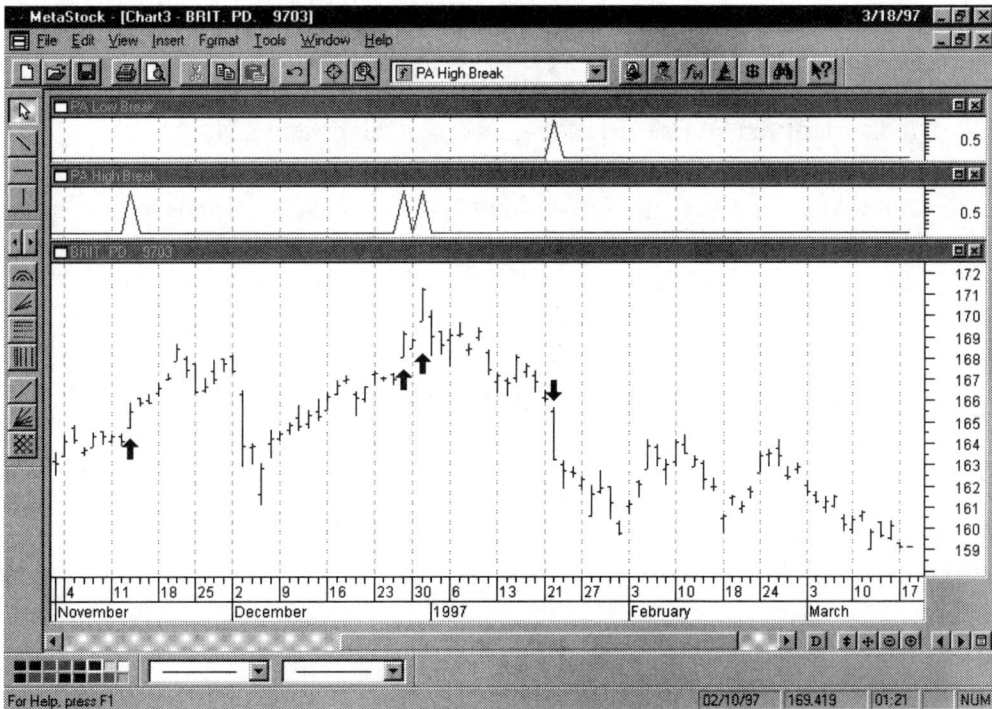

Figure 77. British pound futures. Volatility breakouts automatically identified with the PA High/Low Break system.

Signal Filters

Figure 77 shows a screenshot of the PA High/Low break system. It is not a true trading system, but rather two custom indicators for having *MetaStock* ™ automatically scan hundreds or even thousand of securities for breakouts which can then be further studied for their trade potential. Just the fact of a breakout by itself it not usually reason enough to enter a trade. This is where a signal *filter* comes in. The following custom indicator also checks if the open to close range on the day of the breakout was larger than the open-close range during the last 10 days. If yes, there is a bigger chance that there is "power" behind the move. If not, no signal is generated.

Example

The High Break indicator formula *(MetaStock)*:
C>Ref(HHV(H,20),-1) AND C-O>(Ref(HHV(C-O,10),-1))

The Low Break indicator formula *(MetaStock)*:
C<Ref(LLV(L,20),-1) AND O-C>(Ref(HHV(O-C,10),-1))

These formulas do the following: see if the close is higher/lower than the highest high/lowest low of the last 20 days AND check if the open-close range is larger than the range of the last 10 days. This part of the formula insures that the "move" on the day of the breakout has some significance. By changing these two values the system can be fine-tuned to one's particular trading style.

Another way to filter signals would be to only consider signals in the direction of the overall index/industry segment trend or adding an indicator, like a moving average.

Enhancing Profitability

So far we have focused our attention on trading system elements like studies and indicators. To trade successfully there a few other aspects that must be considered, which do not necessarily require a mechanical trading system at all, even though they could be incorporated into one.

Trading multiple contracts

Trading multiple contracts refers to commodities but the principle applies to stock trading as well. Of course, trading multiple futures contracts is not for everybody since considerable exposure is involved. The idea is to enter and exit trades in steps, rather than all at once. The following examples will serve to illustrate the benefits of this.

Example

A trader decides to go long a certain stock because of a range breakout, but is uncertain about the trade's further potential. The trader has an account size that warrants buying 1000 shares of this stock. Instead of buying all 1000 the day after the breakout, the trader only buys 500. If the market continues moving higher up a day or two later (and the possibility of a false breakout has diminished), the trader goes long the second 500 shares.

The benefit of entering a trade in 2 steps should be clear. If the breakout happens to be a false one (always a possibility), the trade will be stopped out with only half the loss. Remember that keeping losses small is one of the most important rules. If the trader is certain that the breakout is the beginning of a serious move, however, the entire lot should be bought at once.

Example

A trader went long 4 corn contracts at 310. Corn is now trading at, say, 321. Although a long time adage states that you must "let your profits run," it is also true that only a realized profit is a true profit. Markets can turn around very quickly and prices could be back at 310 only 2 days later. The right way to handle this type of situation is as follows (assuming again that you have the account size required to trade multiple contracts): sell one contract now to lock in some profits. This will pay for commissions and leave some over. Tighten the stops on the remaining 3 contracts to 319. The next day the market goes up like a rocket to 327. Now sell another contract, since it is always wise to cash in on windfall profits. With 2 contracts remaining one has option to stay for the long haul by keeping the stops low (at the 319 level, allowing for some adverse action) and hoping that the market will move even higher. If the market now heads south, stopping you out, you will have at least profited somewhat.

Note that there are no perfect ways to exit a trade. The above example just shows one approach how exiting a trade can be handled. Every trader must find a method that suits him/her best. Bollinger Bands can provide some help with finding spots where to take profits.

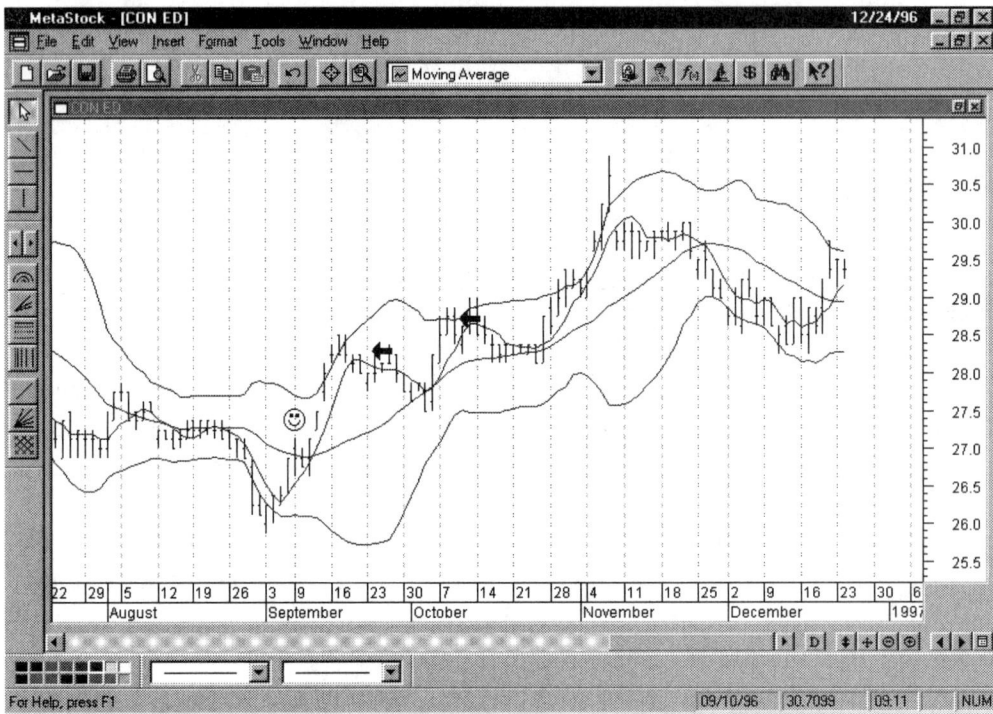

Figure 78. Chart of Con Ed with Bollinger Bands and a 5 day moving average. Right after prices move back from the outer band is often a good place to exit part of a trade and take some profits (assuming a long trade is entered on the bar next to the smiley face).

Waiting for a setup

Waiting for a setup is a rather difficult thing for a novice to do since it entails knowing what to wait for! A setup is a trading situation where the odds are very much in favor of a certain move. It's the kind of situation where an experienced trader's gut feeling tells him that "this is it."

124

Example

A market made a triple top, stochastics have a bearish divergence, a trendline was broken and even the fundamentals have turned negative. These low-risk, high-probability trades only come around every so often, but they are worth waiting for. Problem is, many traders don't have the patience to wait. Most waste their time and energy with questionable or marginal trades and when the big one comes along they are not ready!

The best way to get an eye for setups is by examining charts, lots of them. It will probably take a year or more until the subconscious mind has assimilated enough information to turn on the gut-alarm when the right chart comes along. In fact, one way to design trading systems is by finding interesting chart situations and then seeing which indicator, or combination of studies, can be used to automatically identify that particular "setup."

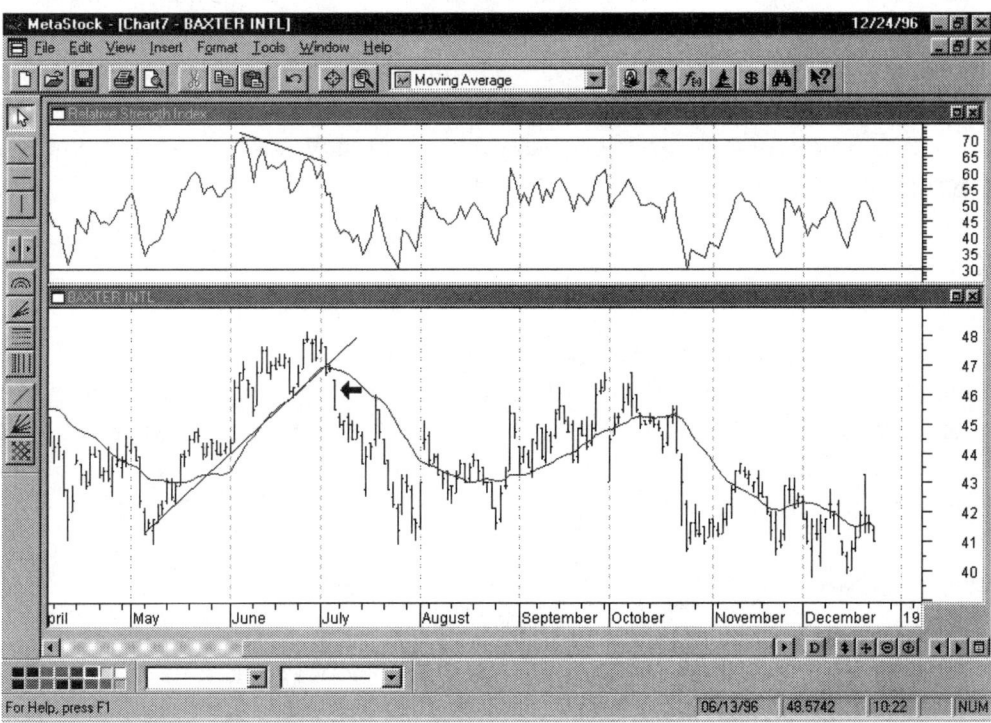

Figure 79. Example of a setup. Bearish divergence on the RSI with four peaks, price breaks the 20-day MA, the trendline and makes a 20 day low (volatility breakout).

How much to risk

During the course of this book the importance of money management has been stressed repeatedly. The term money management includes all monetary aspects of trading like deciding on the portion of trading capital to risk on each trade, adjusting position size according to market volatility, where to place stops and when to take profits. Several books on the market deal exclusively with just these topics. All we can do here is cover the concepts involved and point you in the right direction.

As a general rule one should not risk more than 2-3% of a trading account on any single commodity trade, and no more than 5-7% on an individual stock or mutual fund. In fact, many futures traders I have interviewed only risk 1% per trade. As mentioned earlier in the book, even experienced traders can be hit by a string of losers. To have 10 losing trades in a row (not even that unusual) can mean the end to a trading career if 10%, or more, is risked on a trade. Risking 2% per trade and having 10 losers in a row means that 80% of trading capital will still be available, so one can stay in the game for much longer. What it all boils down to is who it takes money to make money, even with trading. Yes, there are traders that have turned a few thousand dollars into millions, and there are people who won the lottery jackpot two times! It doesn't mean that they possess "secret" knowledge or have crystal ball, they are just very lucky.

Example

In order to make a living trading commodities, say $100,000 per year, will require a trading account of at least $500,000, since it is very unlikely to make more than a 20% return. Do not forget that only money one can afford to lose should be traded, which means that your net worth should be well over $1 million if trading for a living is your goal.

Example

With a stock trading account of $10,000 one should not risk more than $700 (7% of 10,000) on any single trade.

Example

With a commodity trading account of $10,000 one should not risk more than $200-300 on any single trade. This account size automatically disqualifies one from trading most commodities since many major markets have average daily ranges several times that amount and the chance of getting stopped out right after entering a trade is very high.

Placing protective stops

Trading without a stop is like walking down Broadway with your pants down. It is just a matter of time until you get shafted. The decision where to place the stop-loss must be made at the same time when entering a trade is contemplated. If it looks like you would have to risk more than your money management allows then just step back and wait for the next opportunity. It takes some self-discipline to be able to step away from a trade that looks great but where the risk-reward ratio doesn't fit. Always place the stop-loss order along with the order to open a position. Don't fool yourself into believing that you are able to "monitor" the market and pull the plug when necessary. Chances are you will lose much more this way.

There are no absolute rules as to where the stops should be placed. In fact, placing them around obvious support/resistance levels is pretty pointless, as professional traders are very aware of them and often force prices to these levels to trigger buy and sell orders. Testing done by system developers I am associated with has shown that risking a simple dollar amount, based on a market's average daily range and volatility, works just as well as anything else. See the previous chapter, *How much to risk*, for guidelines on this. Even expert traders like John Bollinger have told me that after years of trading they have not found a "one size fits all" stop loss technique. Just as there is no best place to put a stop, there is no perfect kind of stop either. A SCO (Stop Close Only) can avoid you from being stopped out by intraday spikes, but is extremely dangerous in the event of a big move. I like to use simple stops. When it's time to get out you want to get out as quickly as possible, that is why a stop-limit order often works out to be penny wise (by trying to force the market to give you a good price) and dollar foolish (when your order isn't filled at all).

Using trailing stops is the best way to lock in profits once a trade has moved in your direction. A trailing stop is a stop that is adjusted every day or so, depending on how much the market has moved. It enables you to stay with the trade as long as possible (remember that successful trading depends on catching the big moves) while locking in profits. Be sure to tell your broker that you want to do a Cancel-Replace when adjusting your trailing stop. A broker cannot read your mind and only follows your orders. Forgetting to cancel a standing order can result in surprise fills.

Example

A trader buys IBM at 100. The initial stop-loss order is at 95. When the stock rises to 107 the trader cancels the order to sell at 95 and replaces it with an order to sell at 104 on a stop. Assuming IBM rises further to 110 (without going below 104 in the meantime) the trader again adjusts the stop by canceling the order to sell at 104 and replace it with a sell stop at 106.

Although not a straightforward protective stop, an OCO (Order Cancels Order) combination of a stop and limit order can be useful under certain circumstances. Note that some exchanges don't accept OCOs. The idea is to be stopped out if the market turns against you OR close the position at a predetermined profit level, whichever happens first. When would such an approach be appropriate?

Example

A trader bought a gold contract at 380. One day a report is scheduled to be released which he expects to be very bullish for gold. He knows from experience that gold often rises 10 dollars during one trading session on such occasions, but rarely closes up that high. If the report is bearish, the trader doesn't want to lose more than 2 dollars. He calls his broker to place an OCO: *On an OCO sell one January gold at 378 on a stop or at 390 or better.*

Just like one can never know what to expect to the downside (events working against you), there can be surprise developments in favor of a trade. These explosive rallies often only last a day or two, too short a time for many traders to react upon. A good technique to catch profits like this is to have an order in the market which is far away from current prices that will hopefully, with some luck, get executed.

Pyramiding

Pyramiding is not a technique recommended for beginners, but is nevertheless a technique traders should be aware of. The concept is, just like the name implies, that a trade is started out with a large base (several contracts in the case of futures or X amount of shares in the case of stocks). If the trade continues favorably the position is increased by a smaller amount each time, just like building a pyramid. Traders can achieve large profits using this technique, if the market is kind enough to continue to move in the right direction, of course. Unfortunately, some traders pyramid the wrong way. They start out small and add larger stakes, just like an upside-down pyramid. The reason why trading this way is deadly follows.

Example

A trader buys 100 shares of Exxon at 30, 200 more at 35 and 400 more at 40. A decline to 34 will result in a loss of $2200 (400-200-2400). A trader that bought

400 at 30, 200 at 35 and 100 at 40 however will still be $600 in the black (1600-400-600) if prices retreat to 34. Pyramiding the wrong way exposes a disproportionate amount of the total position to adverse market moves.

Trading the equity curve

Any trading system has phases when performance is satisfactory and phases resulting in drawdowns. Remember that market behavior can change in a way that can foul any system. A simple but relatively unknown way to avoid some of these periods is to abstain from using a system when performance is poor. Sounds like a great concept – only trade the winners! This would be too good to be true, of course, but trading the equity curve can be useful nevertheless. Essentially the equity line is used as a "chart," combining it with an indicator or study, just like an ordinary line chart. Most commonly moving averages are employed.

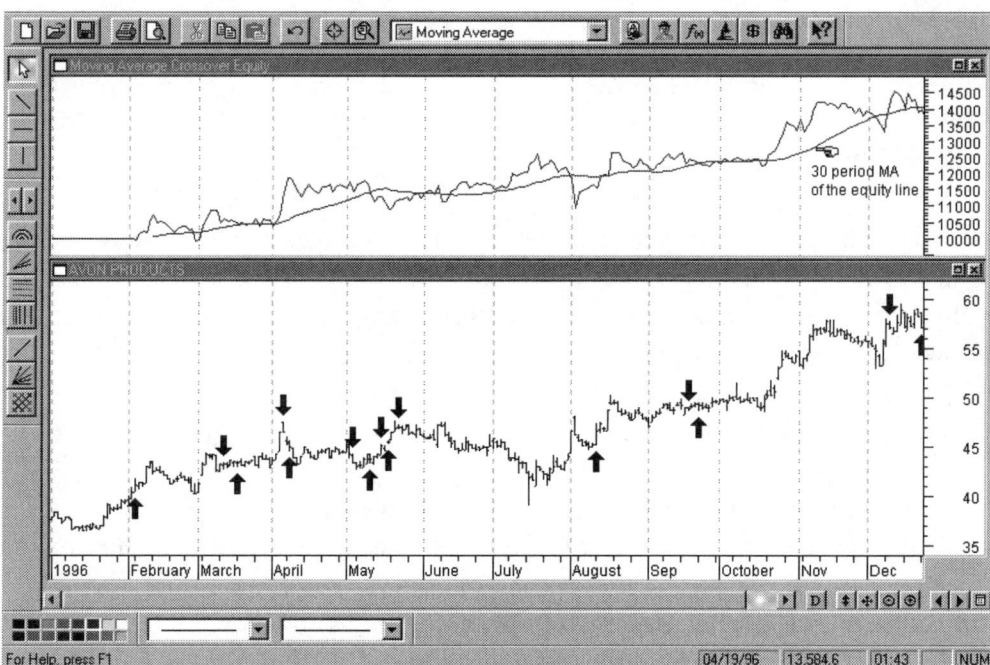

Figure 80. Chart of Avon with a system based on moving average crossovers (MA lines are not visible). The upper chart shows the system's equity curve on top of which a 30 period moving average (of the equity curve itself, not the share prices) is plotted. As long as the slope of the moving average is up or flat the sytem is doing OK.

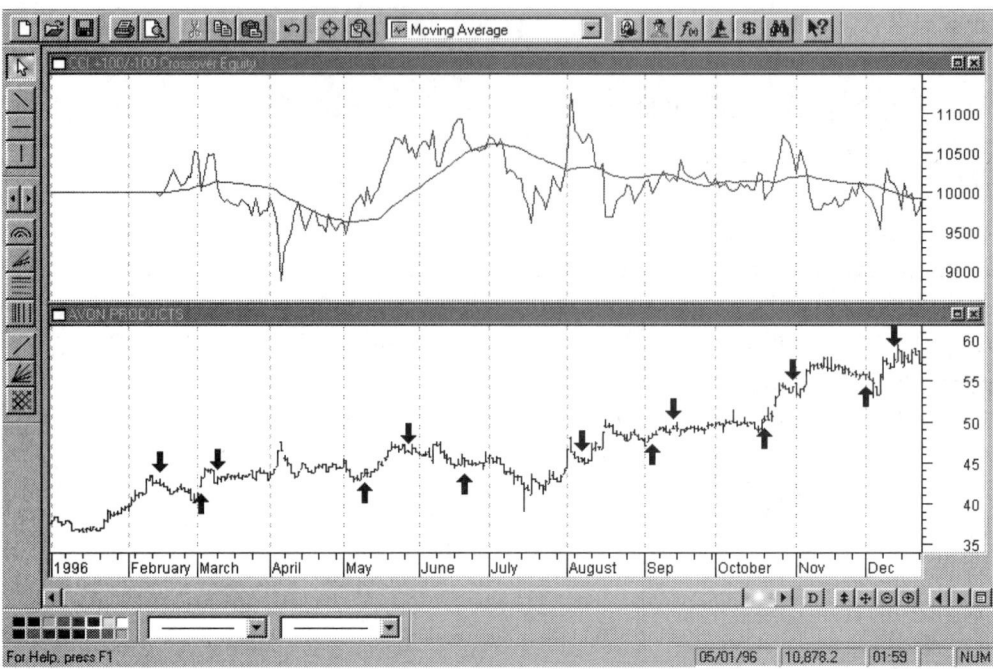

Figure 81. Chart of Avon with a system based on CCI crossover. The performance is much worse compared to the previous example. Note how the equity curve moving average has a downward slope most of the time.

The 30 period moving average of the equity curve used in Figures 80 and 81 is just to illustrate the technique involved. One is free to experiment with other values, or even two separate moving averages. Other studies and indicators might be worth looking into as well.

How to back test

Once a system has been programmed with rules for entries, exits and stops, a process called back testing is performed. As demonstrated earlier with our moving average crossover system, the purpose is to see how a system might have performed in the past. While past performance does not guarantee future results it is even less likely that a system that was never profitable will suddenly show great performance. Back testing should be done on two sets of data, the historical prices that the system is tested with during the design phase and an "out of sample" set of data which the system "does not know." Especially systems that contain some degree of optimization have to be double-checked this way to avoid bad surprises when actually trading.

Example

A trader is designing a system that trades currency futures. For the design process he is using historical data from 1993-1995. During three years one can assume that markets have gone through all typical phases like sideways, bullish and bearish trends. The data from 1996 is kept in reserve and is not used for the moment. After some experimentation and optimization, the trader notices that a system using a 9 &18 day moving average crossover shows good results. If tests with the 1996 data show similarly positive results, the system is likely to be dependable for the intermediate term.

Case Study 3: A Complete Trading System

Putting it all together - entries, stops, & exits

The last case study will attempt to combine many of the techniques and topics covered during previous chapters. It should be regarded as a basis for further learning, experimentation and development. This is a trend following system based on a moving average/breakout combination, whereby the breakout (which is not a range or volatility breakout as covered previously) is actually a filter, or rule, to help reduce bad entries. It is based on an article published by David Landry in the December 1996 issue of *Stocks & Commodities* magazine.

Why we are using moving averages once again and not some terribly complicated custom indicator is simple: they work just as well as anything else. There is no *Holy Grail,* a study that will make you rich because it works every time. Even if you spent months reinventing the wheel by designing your own indicator, chances are 99.9% that it won't work better than anything already in use. RSI & Stochastics are other basic indicators favored by many of the top traders interviewed.

This time we will use an exponential moving average, the kind that lends more weight to recent price history. The time parameter is 20 days, which approximates one month's trading. As mentioned earlier, many markets seem to have cyclical tendencies related to this. Moving average systems are prone to whipsaws which is why we used a second moving average as a filter in our first case study. This time, however, we will employ a breakout filter.

The concept is actually very simple: for a valid long signal to be generated prices must close above the 20 day MA two days in a row. In addition, the lows of these two days are not allowed to touch the MA. A short signal is valid when prices close below the MA two days in a row and the highs of these two days do not touch the MA. The logic behind this filter is: if prices close beyond the MA two days in a row without touching it, the chance of a whipsaw is less likely. As a further precaution the order to enter the trade is placed a bit above/below the highest high/ lowest low of the two days. The stop-loss order when putting the trade on is somewhere below the MA line. If this would risk more than your money management allows, then wait at the sidelines for the next opportunity. As soon as the trade develops favorably move the stop to breakeven (entry price plus a few ticks for commission). This system works best with markets that have strong trending tendencies, like certain stocks and currencies. Another way to filter any kind of daily trend following system is to first analyze the "big picture" by looking at the same security's weekly chart. If the weekly trend is up (use trendlines, moving averages, etc. just like with daily charts) then only long trades with the daily system are taken.

Figure 82. Chart of Amoco with a 20-day exponential moving average. Note how the first arrow points to a bearish alert. The day after the arrow, prices do not get lower than the lowest low of the two days, so nothing is done. The second arrow points to a bullish alert. The day after the arrow, prices do go higher than the highest high of the two days, so a long trade is entered.

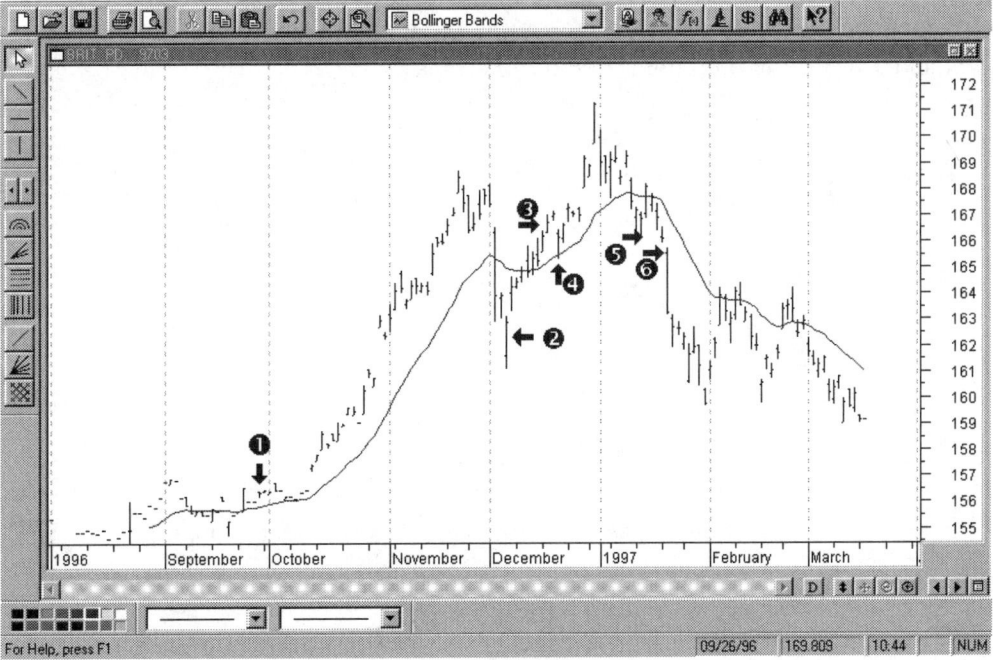

Figure 83. Chart of British Pound.

Figure 83 shows the entry signals the system would have generated with a British Pound contract. A trade is put on at point 1 and is almost stopped out a few days later. Point 2 is a two-day alert to the downside, which is not confirmed the next day with a lower low. At point 3 the system goes long by buying at the open after a two-day bullish alert. This trade is stopped out at a loss two days later when prices penetrate the MA at point 4. At point 5 is the second day of a bearish alert, which is not followed up by a lower low the next day. Point 7 points to the entry at the open after a two-day bearish alert.

With a trading approach as the system described here it is not a good idea to stay with a trade until another signal is generated, thus always having a position. Although most beginners think that the entry part of a trade is the most difficult decision, experienced traders will tell you that finding good exits is much more difficult. As mentioned earlier, once a trade has become profitable trailing stops are advised to conserve profits. Just look at the beautiful trend caught with the trade entered at point 1. It would really hurt if a big portion of profit was lost on a day like the one in December when prices gapped lower and went way below the moving average. Then again, there is no absolute foolproof method of preserving profit with a trailing stop while avoiding being stopped by short corrections at the same time. With trading it is impossible to get everything right all the time. This is a fact that one has to learn to accept from the very start.

A well-designed trading system is programmed with exit rules that are totally separate from the entry rules. The formulas and techniques used can be very complex and are well beyond the scope of this book.

Conclusion

The KISS principle: Keep it Simple Stupid

Traders often believe that a profitable trading system necessitates complex custom indicators, mainframe computers and several live data feeds. While this may be true for certain forms of arbitrage, where minutes and seconds do count, a trader can make money in the markets just as well using basic charting techniques and common indicators. Note: Arbitrage is a form of trading based on taking advantage of slight imbalances between markets. This is the realm of banks and large institutions and does indeed require a major investment in technology.

As there is no, and never will be, a magic formula for guaranteed success, one might as well save some valuable time by concentrating on basic, straightforward approaches. In fact, one of the world's most successful commodity funds, *Hasenbichler Commodities*, employs simple trend following strategies but has very sophisticated money management schemes in place. One of that fund's secrets is that they always have positions in a wide variety of markets, usually 15-30, including U.S., European and Asian exchanges. The reason for this is that the more markets a trader is active in, the likelier it is to catch big trends. It's like going fishing with several rods instead of just one. You will lose more bait but you will also catch some fish!

This kind of diversification is beyond the means of most individual traders, but the point being made here is that success does not depend on the complexity of a system's indicators. What counts in the end is the bottom line. If you are making money in the markets by basing your trading decisions on trendlines alone, fine! If you do great with stocks but not with commodities, then stick to trading stocks. But if trading is giving you sleepless nights (probably because you didn't heed the advice given throughout this book), close your account and put your money into CD's. After all, if you are not enjoying doing something, why bother?

APPENDIX

Glossary of Technical Analysis Terms

Alpha-Beta Trend Channel

The Alpha-Beta Trend Channel study uses the standard deviation of price variation to establish two trend lines, one above and one below the moving average of a price field. This creates a channel (band) where the great majority of price field values will occur.

Arms Ease of Movement

Developed by Richard W. Arms, Jr., this analysis routine expands on Mr. Arms' Equivolume charting tool by quantifying the shape aspects of the plotted boxes. The purpose of this quantifying is to determine the ease, or lack thereof, with which a particular issue is able to move in one direction or another. The ease with which an issue moves is a product of a ratio between the height (trading range) and width (volume) of the plotted box. In general, a higher ratio results from a wider box and indicates difficulty of movement. A lower ratio results from a narrower box and indicates easier movement. This ratio is then related to a comparison between today's and yesterday's trading-range midpoint values to determine the ease of movement value (EMV). A moving average is then applied to the EMV value - the moving average period can be varied in order to make the EMV flexible as a trading tool.

Average True Range

True range is the greatest of the following differences:

1. Today's high to today's low
2. Today's high to yesterday's close
3. Today's low to yesterday's close

The range is normally the "high - low." However, any time the value of yesterday's close is not within the range of today's bar, rule 2) or rule 3) applies. As with most other indicators, the periodic value is summed and smoothed to create the final indicator.

Bollinger Bands

Bollinger Bands plot trading bands above and below a simple moving average. The standard deviation of closing prices for a period equal to the moving average employed is used to determine the band width. This causes the bands to tighten in quiet markets and loosen in volatile markets. The bands can be used to determine overbought and oversold levels, locate reversal areas, project targets for market moves, and determine appropriate stop levels. The bands are used in conjunction with indicators such as RSI, MACD histogram, CCI and Rate of

Change. Divergences between Bollinger Bands and other indicators show potential action points. As a general guideline, look for buying opportunities when prices are in the lower band, and selling opportunities when the price activity is in the upper band.

Candlestick Charts
Method of drawing stock (or commodity) charts which originated in Japan. Requires the presence of Open, High, Low and Close price data to be drawn. There are two basic types of candles, the white body and the black body. As with regular bar charts, a vertical line is used to indicate the periods (normally daily) high to low. When prices close higher than they opened, a white rectangle is drawn on top of the high-low line. This rectangle originates at the opening price level and extends up toward the closing price. A down day is drawn in black. The combination of several candles results in patterns (with names like "two crows" or "bullish Engulfing Pattern") which give insight into future price activity. For other Japanese charting approaches also see Renko and Kagi charts.

Chaikin Oscillator
The Chaikin Oscillator is created by subtracting a 10 period exponential moving average of the Accumulation/Distribution Line from a 3 period moving average of the Accumulation/Distribution Line.

Commodity Channel Index (CCI)
The CCI is a timing system that is best applied to commodity contracts which have cyclical or seasonal tendencies. CCI does not determine the length of cycles - it is designed to detect when such cycles begin and end through the use of a statistical analysis which incorporates a moving average and a divisor reflecting both the possible and actual trading ranges. Although developed primarily for commodities, the CCI could conceivably be used to analyze stocks as well.
FORMULA: CCI=(M-MAVG)/(0.015xDAVG)
M=1/3 (H+L+C) H=Highest price for a period L=Lowest price for a period
C=Closing price for a period MAVG=N-period simple moving average of M
DAVG= 1/n x SUMi=1 to n (ABS(MI-MAVG))

Commodity Selection Index
The Commodity Selection Index is related to the Directional Movement Index. Whereas the ADXR plot of the DMI is used to rate contracts from the longer term, trend-following point of view, the CSI is used to rate items in the more volatile short term. The Commodity Selection Index takes into account the ADXR from the Directional Movement Index, the Average True Range, the value of a one cent move as well as margin and commission requirements. The higher the CSI rating, the more attractive an item is for trading.

Cutler's RSI

Cutler's RSI is a slight variation of Welles Wilder's original Relative Strength Index. The RSI is a momentum oscillator used to identify overbought and oversold conditions by keying on specific levels, generally 30 and 70, on a chart scaled from 0 to 100. The study can also be used to detect the following:

> · Movement which might not be as readily apparent on the bar chart
> · Failure swings above 70 or below 30 which indicate reversals
> · Support and resistance
> · Divergences between RSI and price

Cutler's RSI is calculated as follows:
> · RSI = 100 - (100 / (1 + RS))
> · RS = UPAV:x / DNAV:x, and . . .
> · UPAV:x = (E, period's Closes UP) / period
> · DNAV:x = (z: period's Closes DOWN) / period
> · A Close UP (or DOWN) = CLOSE - CLOSE previous

If the difference is positive, it is a Close UP. If the difference is negative, the sign is changed and it is a Close DOWN.

Demand Aggregate

The Demand Aggregate is used similarly as the Demand Index, but adds Open Interest as a consideration in the formula. In its simplest terms, the system confirms price trends by analyzing concurrent Volume and Open Interest trends. For example, a rise in price, coupled with rising Volume and Open Interest figures, is considered a bullish indicator. Interpretations are made with respect to the relationship between the movement of Volume, Open Interest, and Price.

Demand Index

The Demand Index is a leading indicator which combines volume and price data in such a way as to indicate a change in price trend. It is designed so that at the very least it is a coincidental indicator, never a lagging one. The calculation of this index is relatively complex. This analysis is based on the general observation that volume tends to peak before prices peak, both in the commodity and stock markets.

Detrend

Detrend is simply another interpretation of a moving average. It provides a means of identifying underlying cycles not apparent when the moving average is viewed in its original form by effectively hiding the major cycles from view. The moving average line is drawn as a straight, horizontal base line on the

Detrend chart. Price bars are then re-positioned along this line depending on their relation to the moving average line.

Directional Movement Index

Directional Movement uses a rather complicated set of calculations designed to rate the directional movement of commodities or stocks on a scale from 0 to 100. For those traders who employ trend-following methods, commodities or stocks rating in the upper end of the scale would be attractive. Those using non-trending methods, commodities or stocks rating at the lower end of the scale should be considered for trading. At its most basic, the Directional Movement would affect trading in the following manner: long positions would be taken when the "+DI" line crosses over the "-DI" line. Short positions would be taken when the "-DI" line crosses over the "+DI" line. Further components of this index are the ADX and ADXR lines.

Elliott Wave

Elliott wave theory goes beyond traditional charting techniques by providing an overall view of market movement that helps explain why and where certain chart patterns develop. The three major aspects of wave analysis are pattern, time and ratio. The basic Elliott pattern consists of a 5 wave uptrend followed by a three wave correction. Each "leg" of a wave in turn consists of smaller waves. Elliott waves can be used to successfully define where the market currently is in relation to "the big picture" but is usually to unreliable for short term trading.

Fibonacci Ratios and Retracements

They can be applied both to price and time, although it is more common to use them on prices. The most common levels used in retracement analysis are 61.8%, 38% and 50%. When a move starts to reverse the 3 price levels are calculated (and drawn using horizontal lines) using a movement's low to high. These retracement levels are then interpreted as likely levels where counter moves will stop. It is interesting to note that the Fibonacci ratios were also known to Greek and Egyptian mathematicians.The ratio was known as the Golden Mean and was applied in music and architecture. A Fibonacci spiral is a logarithmic spiral that tracks natural growth patterns.

Gann Square

The Gann Square is a mathematical system for finding support and resistance based upon a commodity or stock's extreme low or high price for a given period. Attainment of a particular price level in a square tells you the next probable price peak or valley of a future movement. The probable price levels tend to be more reliable if they are extrapolated from Gann Square values along one of the major axes of the Gann Square. The Gann Square is generated from a central value, normally a all-time or cyclical high or low. If a low is used, the numbers are incremented by a constant amount to generate the Gann Square. If a high is used, the numbers are decremented during the square generation.

Haurlan Index

This indicator is calculated daily from the plurality of NYSE advances over declines. There are three components of the Haurlan index: Short Term, Long Term and Intermediate Term.

1) Short Term. A 3-day exponential moving average is taken of the net NYSE advances over declines, measuring the short term condition of the market. When this index moves above +100, a market short term buy signal is generated. The signal is in effect until the market drops below -150 at which time a sell signal is generated. The sell signal remains in effect until the index moves above +100 again.

2) Intermediate Term. Same as above but with a 20-day exponential moving average. This index is considered the most important of the three. Market buys and sells are determined in this index by the crossing of trendlines or support/ resistance levels depending on the particular market in question. For example, when the market is basing out in preparation for an uptrend, a resistance level may be set up. Once its value is determined, buy and sell signals could be generated for that market.

3) Long Term. Same as above except for a 200-day exponential moving average. Useful for determining trends but not for signals.

Herrick Payoff Index

This is a commodity trading tool, useful for the early spotting of changes in price trend direction. The Payoff Index is best used to distinguish trends that are destined to continue from those that will most likely be short-lived. The Payoff Index is a commodity trading tool that is useful in the early identification of changes in the direction of price trends. The Payoff Index frequently helps distinguish between a rally in a trend that is destined to continue and a significant trend change that will provide a worthwhile trading opportunity. The Payoff Index tends to give coincident signals within a day or two before a significant change in price trend. This advance action is accomplished through use of trading volume and contract open interest to modify the price action. Analysts have observed that volume trends often change before a price-trend change. There are also generally accepted relationships between the price trend and the trend of open interest.

Kagi Chart

Like Candlestick and Renko charts, Kagi charts come from Japan and were made popular in the USA by Steve Nison. Kagi charts display a series of connecting vertical lines where the thickness and direction of the lines are dependent on the price action. If closing prices continue to move in the direction of the prior vertical Kagi line, then that line is extended. However, if the closing price reverses by a pre-determined "reversal" amount, a new Kagi line is drawn in the next column in the opposite direction. An interesting aspect of the Kagi chart is that when closing prices penetrate the prior column's high or low, the thickness of the Kagi line changes.

MACD (Moving Average Convergence/Divergence)
The MACD is used to determine overbought or oversold conditions in the market. Written for stocks and stock indices, MACD can be used for commodities as well. The MACD line is the difference between the long and short exponential moving averages of the chosen item. The signal line is an exponential moving average of the MACD line. Signals are generated by the relationship of the two lines. As with RSI and Stochastics, divergences between the MACD and prices may indicate an upcoming trend reversal.

McClellan Oscillator
This index is based on New York Stock Exchange net advances over declines. It provides a measure of such conditions as overbought/oversold and market direction on a short-to- intermediate term basis. The McClellan Oscillator measures a bear market selling climax when it registers a very negative reading in the vicinity of -150. A sharp buying pulse in the market would be indicated by a very positive reading, well above 100.

Momentum
Momentum provides an analysis of changes in prices (as opposed to changes in price levels). Changes in the rate of ascent or descent are plotted. The Momentum line is graphed positive or negative to a straight line representing time. The position of the time line is determined by price at the beginning of the Momentum period. Traders use this analysis to determine overbought and oversold conditions. When a maximum positive point is reached, the market is said to be overbought and a downward reaction is imminent. When a maximum negative point is reached, the market is said to be oversold and an upward reaction is indicated.

Moving Averages
The moving average is probably the best known, and most versatile, indicator in the analyst's tool chest. It can be used with the price of your choice (highs, closes or whatever) and can also be applied to other indicators, helping to smooth out volatility. As the name implies, the Moving Average is the average

of a given amount of data. For example, a 14 day average of closing prices is calculated by adding the last 14 closes and dividing by 14. The result is noted on a chart. The next day the same calculations are performed with the new result being connected (using a solid or dotted line) to yesterday's. And so forth. Variations of the basic Moving Average are the Weighted and Exponential moving averages.

Norton High/Low Indicator

The Norton High/Low Indicator uses results from the Demand Index and the Stochastic study and is designed to pick tops and bottoms on long term price charts. Two lines are generated: the NLP line and the NHP line. The system also uses level lines at -2 and -3. The NLP line crossing -3 to the downside is the signal that a new bottom will occur in 4-6 periods, using daily, weekly, or monthly data. Similarly, the NHP line crossing -3 to the downside indicates a new top in the same time frame. The indicator tends to be more reliable using longer term data (weekly or monthly). When either indicator drops below the - 3 level, a reversal may be imminent. The reversal (or hook) is the signal to enter the market. For greater reliability, use the Norton High/Low Indicator together with other studies for confirmation.

Notis %V

A way to measure volatility is to measure the daily ranges between the high and the low. Volatility is high when the daily range is large and low when the daily range is small. The Notis %V study contains two separate indicators. It divides market volatility into upward and downward components (UVLT and DVLT). Both are plotted separately in the same window, and can be plotted as an oscillator. The upward component is also compared to the total volatility (UVLT + DVLT) and expressed as a percentage; thus the name, %V. Volatility can be a key to options trading. A good sense of market volatility can help you avoid those frustrating times when the market moves your way but your option still loses value.

On Balance Volume (OBV)

OBV is one of the most popular volume indicators and was developed by Joseph Granville. Constructing an OBV line is very simple: the total volume for each day is assigned a positive or negative value depending on whether prices closed higher or lower that day. A higher close results in the volume for that day to get a positive value, while a lower close results in negative value. A running total is kept by adding or subtracting each day's volume based on the direction of the close. The direction of the OBV line is the thing to watch, not the actual volume numbers.

Formula: OBV=SUM(C-CP)/(ABS(C-CP)xV)
C=Today's Close CP=Yesterday's Close V=Today's Volume

Parabolic (SAR)

The Parabolic is a Time/Price system for the automatic setting of stops. The stop is both a function of price and of time. The system allows a few days for market reaction after a trade is initiated after which stops begin to move in more rapid incremental daily amounts in the direction the trade was initiated. For example, when a long position is taken the stop will move up regardless of price direction. However, the distance that the stop moves up is determined by the favorable distance the price has moved. If the price fails to move favorably within a certain period of time, the stop reverses the position and begins a new time period.

Point & Figure Charts

The Point and Figure (PF) charting method is a technique that has been used for many years in analyzing the variations in prices of stocks and commodities. There are several types of P & F charting methods. Some employ trend lines, resistance levels, and various other additions to the chart. In this study, we shall be concerned with only daily reversal type charts. The principal advantage of a P & F chart is that it is much easier to read and interpret than other types of charts. All the small, and often confusing, price movements are eliminated, and only the most important features of the price action remain. It would be reasonable to think of this method as a filter that (hopefully) allows only meaningful information to enter the chart and ultimately the decision process. Two basic symbols are used:

> **X** Denotes the continuance of an increase in price and is always "stacked" in the vertical direction.
> **O** Denotes the continuance of a decrease in price and is always "stacked" in the vertical direction.

While prices are rising X's are used. When falling, O's are used. They are always plotted on rectangular grid graph paper such that columns of X's and O's alternate. A Point and Figure chart is characterized by the specification of two parameters: box size and reversal number. The box size dictates the price range associated with a particular box (cubical area within the grid), while the reversal number specifies the conditions which terminate a column of X's and begin a column of O's and vice-versa.

Price Patterns

Price Patterns are formations which appear on commodity and stock charts which have shown to have a certain degree of predictive value. Some of the most common patterns include: Head & Shoulders (bearish), Inverse Head &

Shoulders (bullish), Double Top (bearish), Double Bottom (bullish), Triangles, Flags and Pennants (can be bullish or bearish depending on the prevailing trend).

Random Walk Index

This indicator is defined as the ratio of an actual price move to the expected random walk. If the move is greater than a random walk, and thus a trend is present, its index will be larger that 1.0.

Rate of Change

Rate of Change is used to monitor momentum by making direct comparisons between current and past prices on a continual basis. The results can be used to determine the strength of price trends. Note: This study is the same as the Momentum except that Momentum uses subtraction in its calculations while Rate of Change uses division. The resulting lines of these two studies operated over the same data will look exactly the same - only the scale values will differ.

RSI - Relative Strength Index

This indicator was developed by Welles Wilder Jr. Relative Strength is often used to identify price tops and bottoms by keying on specific levels (usually "30" and "70") on the RSI chart which is scaled from from 0-100. The study is also useful to detect the following:

> Movement which might not be as readily apparent on the bar chart
> Failure swings above 70 or below 30 which can warn of coming reversals
> Support and resistance levels
> Divergence between the RSI and price which is often a useful reversal indicator

The Relative Strength Index requires a certain amount of lead-up time in order to operate successfully. The formula for calculating the RSI is:

$$rsi=100-(100/1-rs)$$

rs= average of x day's up closes divided by average of x day's down closes

Renko Chart

The Renko charting method probably got its name from "renga," which is the Japanese word for bricks. Introduced by Steve Nison, a well-known authority on the Candlestick charting method, Renko charts are similar to Three Line Break charts except that in a Renko chart, a line is drawn in the direction of the prior move only if a fixed amount (i.e., the box size) has been exceeded. The bricks are always equal in size. Example: With a five unit Renko chart, a 20 point rally is displayed as four equally sized, five unit high Renko bricks.

Stochastic

The Stochastic Indicator is based on the observation that as prices increase, closing prices tend to accumulate ever closer to the highs for the period. Conversely, as prices decrease, closing prices tend to accumulate ever closer to the lows for the period. Trading decisions are made with respect to divergence between % of "D" (one of the two lines generated by the study) and the item's price. For example, when a commodity or stock makes a high, reacts, and subsequently moves to a higher high while corresponding peaks on the % of "D" line make a high and then a lower high, a bearish divergence is indicated. When a commodity or stock has established a new low, reacts, and moves to a lower low while the corresponding low points on the % of "D" line make a low and then a higher low, a bullish divergence is indicated. Traders act upon this divergence when the other line generated by the study (K) crosses on the right-hand side of the peak of the % of "D" line in the case of a top, or on the right-hand side of the low point of the % of "D" line in the case of a bottom. Two variations of the Stochastic Indicator are in use: Regular and Slow. When the Regular plot of the Stochastic is too choppy, the "Slow" version can often clarify the results by reducing the sensitivity of the calculations. The formula is:

Note: 5 Days is the most commonly used value for %K

$$\%K = 100 \{(C-L5)/(H5-L5)\}$$

The %D line is a 3 day smoothed version of the %K line
$\%D = 100(H3/L3)$ where H3 is the 3 day sum of (C-L5) and L3 is the 3 day sum of (H5-L5)

Stoller STARC Bands

STARC bands create a channel surrounding a simple moving average. The width of the created channel varies with a period of the average range; thus the name ('ST' for Stoller, plus 'ARC' for Average Range Channel). STARC Bands, in a fashion similar to Bollinger Bands, will tighten in steady markets and loosen in volatile markets. However, rather than being based on closes, the STARC Bands are based on the average true range, thus giving a more in depth picture of the market volatility. While the penetration of a Bollinger Band may indicate a continuation of a price move, the STARC Bands define upper and lower limits for normal price action.

Swing Index

The Swing Index (primarily for use with commodity trading) attempts to determine real market direction, and changes in direction, by making use of the most significant comparisons between the results (Open-High-Low-Close) of the current and previous days' trading.

Time Cycles

Some analysts believe that price analysis alone only offers half the information needed for successful trading. The other part is time, more exactly time cycles, which give actual insight into understanding the movements of markets. Common cycles are the seasonal cycles apparent in many commodity markets, but cycles can be detected on intraday charts as well.

Trading Index

This index (also kown as the "Arms" index, or "TRIN") measures the relative strength of volume associated with advancing stocks against the strength of volume associated with declining stocks. When used as a short term indicator, readings below 1.0 are considered bullish while readings above 1.0 are considered bearish. An extreme bearish reading would be 1.5 or higher; an extreme bullish reading would be .5 and lower. Readings of 2.0 or .3 would be considered "climactic." For the intermediate term, a bearish sign is an index over 1.0, bullish under 1.0. For the long term, the Trading Index can be viewed as an overbought / oversold indicator.

Trix

Single linear exponential smoothing was developed in the early 1950s as a means of prediction along a straight line whose slope was based on previous data. The Triple Exponential Smoothing Oscillator (Trix) has now been developed to act on trends of a higher order than linear. Trix uses a one-day momentum of a triple exponential smoothed price series to produce an indicator which is cycle dependent. Changes in the Trix direction are less prone to whipsaws than standard cycle-momentum indicators. The period is chosen to filter out any insignificant cycles shorter than the period. Fourier Analysis or visual observation may be used to find the proper cycle length of a given market. Raising the number of days will remove more small cycles and smooth out the oscillator, but at the loss of sensitivity. The more smoothing that is applied to the data, the more of a lag in the oscillator, but not nearly the lag of a normal moving average.

Volume Accumulation

This volume indicator addresses some of On Balance Volume's shortcomings and was developed by Marc Chaikin. Where OBV assigns all of a day's volume a positive or negative value, Volume Accumulation counts only a percentage of the volume as positive or negative, depending on where the close is in relation to the average price of the day. The only time the entire day's volume is assigned a positive value is when the close is the same as the day's high. The opposite applies for a close at the day's low.

Volatility

This analysis is based on the idea that stocks bottom from "panic" selling, after which a rebound is imminent. One way of measuring this phenomenon is to observe a widening range between high and low prices each day. In general a progressively wider range, observed over a relatively short period of time, can indicate that a bottom is near. Price tops are generally reached at a more leisurely pace and can be characterized by a narrowing of the price range. This measure of the trading range takes place over a specified period in order to determine whether or not an issue is being "dumped" and is approaching a bottom. A prerequisite to a valid bottom is an increase in the volatility line above the reference line. In a similar manner, an indication of an imminent top would be a decrease in the volatility line below the reference line. As long as volatility is rising, in all probability a stock will not approach a top. It should be noted that this study should be used in conjunction with trend following analyses and momentum oscillators for confirmation and accuracy.

Financial Glossary

ALPHA

A measure of selection risk (also known as residual risk) of a mutual fund in relation to the market. A positive alpha is the extra return awarded to the investor for taking a risk, instead of accepting the market return. For example, an alpha of 0.4 means the fund outperformed the market-based return estimate by 0.4 %. -0.6 means a fund's monthly return was 0.6 % less than would have been predicted from the change in the market alone.

ALPHA EQUATION

The alpha of a fund is determined as follows:
[(sum of y) - ((b)(sum of x))] / n
where: n =number of observations (36 mos)
b = beta of the fund
x = rate of return for the S&P 500
y = rate of return for the fund

AMERICAN DEPOSITORY RECEIPTS

Certificates issued by a U.S. Depository Bank, representing foreign shares held by the bank, usually by a branch or correspondent in the country of issue. One ADR may represent a portion of a foreign share, one share or a bundle of shares of a foreign corporation. If the ADR's are "sponsored," the corporation provides financial information and other assistance to the bank and may subsidize the administration of the ADR's. "Unsponsored" ADR's do not receive such assistance. ADR's carry the same currency, political and economic risks as the underlying foreign share; the prices of the two, adjusted for the SDR/ordinary ratio, are kept essentially identical by arbitrage. American Depository Shares (ADS) are a similar form of certification.

AMERICAN-STYLE OPTION

An option contract that can be exercised at any time between the date of purchase and the expiration date. Most exchange-traded options are American style.

ANALYST

Employee of a brokerage or fund management house who studies companies and makes buy and sell recommendations on their stocks. Most specialize in a specific industry.

ANNUAL REPORT

Yearly record of a publicly held company's financial condition. It includes a description of the firm's operations, its balance sheet and income statement. SEC rules require that it be distributed to all shareholders. A more detailed version is called a 10-K.

ARBITRAGE

Profiting from differences in the price of a single security that is traded on more than one market.

ARMS INDEX

Also known as TRading INdex (TRIN):= #advancing issues/#declining issues
        Total up volume/total down volume
An advance/decline market indicator. Less than 1.0 indicates bullish demand, while above 1.0 is bearish. The index often is smoothed with a simple moving average.

ASSIGNMENT

The receipt of an exercise notice by an options writer that requires him to sell (in the case of a call) or purchase (in the case of a put) the underlying security at the specified strike price.

AT THE MONEY

An option is at-the-money if the strike price of the option is equal to the market price of the underlying security. For example, if xyz stock is trading at 54, then the xyz 54 option is at-the-money.

AUTOREGRESSIVE

Using previous data to predict future data.

AVERAGE

An arithmetic mean of selected stocks intended to represent the behavior of the market or some component of it. One good example is the widely quoted Dow Jones Industrial Average, which adds the current prices of the 30 DJIA's stocks, and divides the results by a predetermined number, the divisor.

AVERAGE MATURITY

The average time to maturity of securities held by a mutual fund. Changes in interest rates have greater impact on funds with longer average life.

BACK OFFICE

Brokerage house clerical operations that support, but do not include, the trading of stocks and other securities. Includes all written confirmation and settlement of trades, record keeping and regulatory compliance.

BANKER'S ACCEPTANCE

A short-term credit investment created by a non-financial firm and guaranteed by a bank as to payment. Acceptances are traded at discounts from face value in the secondary market. These instruments have been a popular investment for money market funds.

BASIS

The price an investor pays for a security plus any out-of-pocket expenses. It is used to determine capital gains or losses for tax purposes when the stock is sold.

BASIS POINTS

Refers to yield on bonds. Each percentage point of yield in bonds equals 100 basis points. If a bond yield changes from 7.25 % to 7.39 %, that's a rise of 14 basis points.

BEAR

An investor who believes a stock or the overall market will decline. A bear market is a prolonged period of falling stock prices, usually by 20% or more.

BEAR RAID

A situation in which large traders sell positions with the intention of driving prices down.

BETA (STOCKS)

Measure of a stock's risk in relation to the market. 0.7 means a stock price is likely to move up or down 70% of the market change; 1.3 means the stock is likely to move up or down 30% more than the market.

BETA EQUATION (STOCKS)

The beta of a stock is determined as follows:
[(n) (sum of (xy))]-[(sum of x) (sum of y)]
[(n) (sum of (xx))]-[(sum of x) (sum of x)]

where: n = # of observations (24-60 months)
x = rate of return for the S&P 500 Index
y = rate of return for the stock

BETA (MUTUAL FUNDS)

The measure of a fund's risk in relation to the market. 0.7 means the fund's total return is likely to move up or down 70% of the market change; 1.3 means total return is likely to move up or down 30% more than the market.

BETA EQUATION (MUTUAL FUNDS)

The beta of a fund is determined as follows:

[(n) (sum of (xy))]-[(sum of x) (sum of y)]
[(n) (sum of (xx))]-[(sum of x) (sum of x)]

where: n = # of observations (36 months)
x = rate of return for the S&P 500 Index
y = rate of return for the fund

BLOW-OFF TOP

A steep and rapid increase in price followed by a steep and rapid drop in price. This is an indicator seen in charts and used in technical analysis of stock price and market trends.

BREAKOUT

A rise in a security's price above a resistance level (commonly its previous high price) or drop below a level of support (commonly the former lowest price). A breakout is taken to signify a continuing move in the same direction. Can be used by technical analysts as a buy or sell indication.

BULL

An investor who thinks the market will rise.

BULL MARKET

A market which is on a consistent upward trend.

BUYOUT

Purchase of a controlling interest (or percent of shares) of a company's stock. A leveraged buyout is done with borrowed money.

CALL OPTION

An option contract that gives the holder of the option the right (but not the obligation) to purchase, and obligates the writer to sell, a specified number of shares of the underlying stock at the given strike price, on or before the expiration date of the contract.

CAPITAL EXPENDITURES
Amount used during a particular period to acquire or improve long term assets such as property, plant, or equipment.

CAPITAL GAIN
When a stock is sold for a profit, it's the difference between the net sales price of securities and their net cost, or original basis. If a stock is sold below cost, the difference is a capital loss.

CAPITAL LOSS
The difference between the net cost of a security and the net sale price, if that security is sold at a loss.

CASH DIVIDEND
A dividend paid in cash to a company's shareholders. The amount is normally based on profitability and is taxable as income. A cash distribution may include capital gains and return of capital in addition to the dividend.

CASH AND EQUIVALENTS
The value of assets that can be converted into cash immediately, as reported by a company. Usually includes bank accounts and marketable securities, such as government bonds and Bankers' Acceptances. Cash equivalents on balance sheets include securities (e.g., notes) that mature within ninety days.

CASH FLOW
In investments, it represents earnings before depreciation amortization and non-cash charges. Sometimes called cash earnings. Cash Flow from operations, called Funds From Operations (FFO) by real estate and other investment trusts, is important because it indicates the ability to pay dividends.

CHANGES IN FINANCIAL POSITION
Sources of funds internally provided from operations which alter a company's cash flow position: depreciation, deferred taxes, other sources, and capital expenditures.

CHURNING
Excessive trading of a client's account in order to increase the broker's commissions.

CLOSING PURCHASE
A transaction in which the purchaser's intention is to reduce or eliminate a short position in a stock, or in a given series of options.

CLOSING SALE

A transaction in which the seller's intention is to reduce or eliminate his long position in a stock, or a given series of options.

COMMISSION

The fee paid to a broker to execute a trade, based on number of shares, bonds, options and/or their dollar value. In 1975, deregulation led to the creation of discount brokers, who charge lower commissions than full service brokers. Full service brokers offer advice and usually have a full staff of analysts who follow specific industries. Discount brokers simply execute a client's order—and usually do not offer an opinion on a stock.

COMMON STOCK/OTHER EQUITY

Value of outstanding common shares at par, plus accumulated retained earnings. Also called shareholders' equity.

CONFIDENCE INDICATOR

A measure of investors' faith in the economy and the securities market. A low or deteriorating level of confidence is considered by many technical analysts as a bearish sign.

CONFIRMATION

The written statement that follows any "trade" in the securities markets. Confirmation is issued immediately after a trade is executed. It spells out settlement date, terms, commission, etc.

CONVERGENCE

The movement of the price of a futures contract toward the price of the underlying cash commodity. At the start, the contract price is higher because of the time value. But as the contract nears expiration, the futures price and the cash price converge.

CORNER A MARKET

To purchase enough of the available supply of a commodity or stock in order to manipulate its price.

COUPON RATE

In bonds, notes or other fixed income securities, the stated percentage rate of interest, usually paid twice a year.

COVERED CALL

A short call option position in which the writer owns the number of shares of the underlying stock represented by the option contracts. Covered calls generally limit the risk the writer takes because the stock does not have to be bought at the market price, if the holder of that option decides to exercise it.

COVERED PUT

A put option position in which the option writer also is short the corresponding stock or has deposited, in a cash account, cash or cash equivalents equal to the exercise of the option. This limits the option writer's risk because money or stock is already set aside. In the event that the holder of the put option decides to exercise the option, the writer's risk is more limited than it would be on an uncovered or naked put option.

CURRENT ASSETS

Value of cash, accounts receivable, inventories, marketable securities and other assets that could be converted to cash in less than 1 year.

CURRENT LIABILITIES

Amount owed for salaries, interest, accounts payable and other debts due within 1 year.

CURRENT RATIO

Indicator of short-term debt paying ability. Determined by dividing current assets by current liabilities. The higher the ratio, the more liquid the company.

CURRENT YIELD

For bonds or notes, the coupon rate divided by the market price of the bond.

DAY ORDER

An order to buy or sell stock that automatically expires if it can't be executed on the day it is entered.

DEBT/EQUITY RATIO

Indicator of financial leverage. Compares assets provided by creditors to assets provided by shareholders. Determined by dividing long term debt by common stockholders' equity.

DECILE RANK

Performance over time, rated on a scale of 1-10. 1 indicates that a mutual fund's return was in the top 10% of funds being compared, while 3 means the return was in the top 30%. Objective Rank compares all funds in the same investment strategy category. All Rank compares all funds.

DECLARATION DATE

The date on which a firm's directors meet and announce the date and amount of the next dividend.

DEPRECIATION

A non-cash expense that provides a source of free cash flow. Amount allocated during the period to amortize the cost of acquiring long term assets over the useful life of the assets.

DERIVATIVE SECURITY

A financial security, such as an option or future, whose value is derived in part from the value and characteristics of another security, the underlying security.

DETREND

To remove the general drift, tendency or bent of a set of statistical data as related to time.

DISTRIBUTIONS

Payments from fund or corporate cash flow. May include dividends from earnings, capital gains from sale of portfolio holdings and return of capital. Fund distributions can be made by check or by investing in additional shares. Funds are required to distribute capital gains (if any) to shareholders at least once per year. Some Corporations offer Dividend Reinvestment Plans (DRP).

DIVIDEND REINVESTMENT PLANS (DRP)

Plans offered by many corporations for the reinvestment of dividends, sometimes at a discount from market price, on the dividend payment date. Many DRP's also allow the investment of additional cash from the shareholder. The DRP is usually administered by the company without charges to the holder.

DIVERGENCE

When two or more averages or indices fail to show confirming trends.

DIVIDEND

Distribution of a portion of a company's earnings, cash flow or capital to shareholders, in cash or additional stock.

DIVIDEND YIELD (STOCKS)

Indicated Yield represents annual dividends divided by current stock price.

DIVIDEND YIELD (FUNDS)

Indicated Yield represents return on a share of a mutual fund held over the past 12 months. Assumes fund was purchased 1 year ago. Reflects effect of sales charges (at current rates), but not redemption charges.

DIVIDENDS PER SHARE

Dividends paid for the past 12 months divided by the number of common shares outstanding, as reported by a company. The number of shares often is determined by a weighted average of shares outstanding over the reporting term.

DIVIDEND REINVESTMENT PLAN

Automatic reinvestment of shareholder dividends in more shares of a company's stock, often without commissions. Some plans provide for the purchase of additional shares at a discount to market price. Dividend reinvestment plans allow shareholders to accumulate stock over the long term using dollar cost averaging.

DOWNGRADE

A classic negative change in ratings for a stock, and or other rated security.

EARNINGS

Net income for the company during the period.

EARNINGS PER SHARE (EPS)

Also referred to as Primary Earnings Per Share. Net income for the past 12 months divided by the number of common shares outstanding, as reported by a company. The company often uses a weighted average of shares outstanding over reporting term.

EARNINGS YIELD

The ratio of Earnings Per Share after allowing for tax and interest payments on fixed interest debt, to the current share price. The inverse of the Price/Earnings ratio. It's the Total Twelve Months Earnings divided by number of outstanding shares, divided by the recent price, multiplied by 100. The end result is shown in percentage.

EQUITY

The value of the common stockholders' equity in a company as listed on the balance sheet.

EQUITY OPTIONS

Securities that give the holder the right to buy or sell a specified number of shares of stock, at a specified price for a certain (limited) time period. Typically one option equals 100 shares of stock.

EUROPEAN-STYLE OPTION
An option contract that can only be exercised on the expiration date.

EXCHANGE
The marketplace in which shares, options and futures on stocks, bonds, commodities and indices are traded. Principal US stock exchanges are: New York Stock Exchange (NYSE), American Stock Exchange (AMEX) and the National Association of Securities Dealers (NASDAQ).

EX-DIVIDEND DATE
The first day of trading when the seller, rather than the buyer, of a stock will be entitled to the most recently announced dividend payment. This date set by the NYSE (and generally followed on other US exchanges) is currently two business days before the record date. A stock that has gone ex-dividend is marked with an x in newspaper listings on that date.

EXECUTION
The process of completing an order to buy or sell securities. Once a trade is executed, it is reported by a Confirmation Report; settlement (payment and transfer of ownership) occurs in the U.S. between 1 (mutual funds) and 5 (stocks) days after an order is executed. Settlement times for exchange listed stocks are in the process of being reduced to three days in the U.S.

EXERCISE
To implement the right of the holder of an option to buy (in the case of a call) or sell (in the case of a put) the underlying security.

EXPENSE RATIO
The percentage of the assets that were spent to run a mutual fund (as of the last annual statement). This includes expenses such as management and advisory fees, overhead costs and 12b-1 (distribution and advertising) fees. The expense ratio does not include brokerage costs for trading the portfolio, although these are reported as a percentage of assets to the SEC by the funds in a Statement of Additional Information (SAI). The SAI is available to shareholders on request. Neither the expense ratio or the SAI includes the transaction costs of spreads, normally incurred in unlisted securities and foreign stocks. These two costs can add significantly to the reported expenses of a fund. The expense ratio is often termed an Operating Expense Ratio (OER).

EXPIRATION CYCLE

An expiration cycle relates to the dates on which options on a particular security expire. A given option will be placed in 1 of 3 cycles, the January cycle, the February cycle, or the March cycle. At any point in time, an option will have contracts with 4 expiration dates outstanding, 2 in near-term months and 2 in far-term months.

EXPIRATION DATE

The last day (in the case of American-style) or the only day (in the case of European style) on which an option may be exercised. For stock options, this date is the Saturday immediately following the 3rd Friday of the expiration month; however, brokerage firms may set an earlier deadline for notification of an option holder's intention to exercise. If Friday is a holiday, the last trading day will be the preceding Thursday.

FUND FAMILY

The management company that runs and/or sells shares of the fund. Fund families often offer several funds with different investment objectives.

FUNDS FROM OPERATIONS (FFO)

Used by real estate and other investment trusts to define the cash flow from trust operations. It is earnings with depreciation and amortization added back. A similar term increasingly used is Funds Available for Distribution (FAD), which is FFO less capital investments in trust property and the amortization of mortgages.

FUTURES CONTRACT

Agreement to buy or sell a set number of shares of a specific stock in a designated future month at a price agreed upon by the buyer and seller. The contracts themselves are often traded on the futures market. A futures contract differs from an option because an option is the right to buy or sell, whereas a futures contract is the promise to actually make a transaction.

INDUSTRY

The category describing a company's primary business activity. This usually is determined by the largest portion of revenue.

INITIAL PUBLIC OFFERING (IPO)

A company's first sale of stock to the public. Securities offered in an IPO are often, but not always, those of young, small companies seeking outside equity capital and a public market for their stock. Investors purchasing stock in IPOs generally must be prepared to accept very large risks for the possibility of large gains. IPO's by investment companies (closed end funds) usually contain underwriting fees which represent a load to buyers.

INSIDER INFORMATION
Relevant information about a company that has not yet been made public. It is illegal for holders of this information to make trades based on it, however received.

IN-THE-MONEY
A "call" option is in-the-money if the strike price is less than the market price of the underlying security. A "put" option is in-the-money if the strike price is greater than the market price of the underlying security. For example, an xyz "call" option with a 52 strike price is in-the-money when xyz trades at 52 1/8 or higher. An xyz "put" option with a 52 strike price is in-the-money when xyz is trading at 51 7/8 or lower.

INVENTORY
For companies: raw materials, items available for sale or in the process of being made ready for sale. They can be individually valued by several different means, including cost or current market value, and collectively by FIFO, LIFO or other techniques. The lower value of alternatives is usually used to preclude overstating earnings and assets. For security firms: securities bought and held by a broker or dealer for resale.

INVENTORY TURNOVER
The ratio of annual sales to inventory. Low turnover is an unhealthy sign, indicating excess stocks and/or poor sales.

INVESTMENT TRUST
A closed-end fund regulated by the Investment Company Act of 1940. These funds have a fixed number of shares which are traded on the secondary markets similarly to corporate stocks. The market price may exceed the net asset value per share, in which case it is considered at a "premium." When the market price falls below the NAV/share, it is at a "discount." Many closed end funds are of a specialized nature, with the portfolio representing a particular industry, country, etc. These funds are usually listed on US and foreign exchanges.

IRA/KEOGH ACCOUNTS
Special accounts where you can save and invest, and the taxes are deferred until money is withdrawn. These plans are subject to frequent changes in law with respect to the deductibility of contributions. Withdrawals of tax deferred contributions are taxed as income, including the capital gains from such accounts.

LAST SPLIT

After a stock split, the number of shares distributed for each share held and the date of the distribution.

LIMIT ORDER

An order to buy a stock at or below a specified price or to sell a stock at or above a specified price. For instance, you could tell a broker "buy me 100 shares of XYZ Corp at $15 or less" or to "sell 100 shares of xyz at $12 or better."

LOAD FUND

A mutual fund with shares sold at a price including a sales charge—typically 4% to 8% of the net amount indicated. Some "no-load" funds have distribution fees permitted by Article 12b-1 of the Investment Company Act; these are typically 0.25%. A "true no-load" fund has neither a sales charge nor 12b-1 fee. A load implies that the fund purchaser receives some investment advice or other service worthy of the charge.

LONG POSITION

Occurs when an individual owns securities. An owner of 100 shares of stock is said to be "Long the Stock."

LONG POSITION (OPTIONS)

An options position where a person has executed one or more options trades where the net result is that they are an "owner" or holder of options (i.e., the number of contracts bought exceeds the number of contracts sold).

LONG TERM ASSETS

Value of property, equipment and other capital assets minus the depreciation. This is an entry in the bookkeeping records of a company, usually on a "cost" basis and thus does not necessarily reflect the market value of the assets.

LONG TERM DEBT

Value of obligations of over 1 year that require that interest be paid.

LONG TERM DEBT/CAPITALIZATION

Indicator of financial leverage. Shows long term debt as a proportion of the capital available. Determined by dividing long term debt by the sum of long term debt, preferred stock and common stockholders' equity.

LONG TERM LIABILITIES

Amount owed for leases, bond repayment and other items due after 1 year.

LOW PRICE
The lowest (intraday) price of a stock over a certain period of time.

MANAGEMENT/CLOSELY HELD SHARES
Percentage of shares held by persons closely related to a company, as defined by the Securities and Exchange Commission. Part of these percentages often is included in Institutional Holdings—making the combined total of these percentages over 100. There is overlap as institutions sometimes acquire enough stock to be considered by the SEC to be closely allied to the company.

MARGIN ACCOUNT (STOCKS)
A leverageable account in which stocks can be purchased for a combination of cash and a loan. The loan in the margin account is collateralized by the stock, and if the value of the stock drops sufficiently, the owner will be asked to either put in more cash, or sell a portion of the stock. Margin rules are federally regulated, but margin requirements and interest may vary among broker/dealers.

MARGIN REQUIREMENT (OPTIONS)
The amount of cash an uncovered (naked) option writer is required to deposit and maintain to cover his daily position valuation and reasonably foreseeable intraday price changes.

MARKET CAPITALIZATION
The total dollar value of all outstanding shares. Computed as shares times current market price. It is a measure of corporate size.

MARKET CYCLE
The period between the 2 latest highs or lows of the S&P 500, showing net performance of a fund through both an up and a down market. A market cycle is complete when the S&P is 15% below the highest point or 15% above the lowest point (ending a down market). The dates of the last market cycle are: 12/04/87 to 10/11/90 (low to low).

MARKET ORDER
An order to buy or sell a stock at the going price.

MINIMUM PURCHASES
For mutual funds, the amount required to open a new account (Minimum Initial Purchase) or to deposit into an existing account (Minimum Additional Purchase). These minimums may be lowered for buyers participating in an automatic purchase plan.

MONEY MARKET FUND

A mutual fund that invests only in short term securities, such as bankers' acceptances, commercial paper, repurchase agreements and government bills. The net asset value per share is maintained at $1.00. Such funds are not federally insured, although the portfolio may consist of guaranteed securities and/or the fund may have private insurance protection.

MUTUAL FUND

An open end investment company that pools investors' money to invest in a variety of stocks, bonds, or other securities. A mutual fund issues and redeems shares to meet demand, and the redemption value per share is the net asset value per share, less in some cases a redemption fee which represents a rear-end load. A closed end fund, often incorrectly called a mutual fund, is instead an investment trust. Both are investment companies regulated by the Investment Company Act of 1940.

NET ASSET VALUE (NAV)

The value of a fund's investments. For a mutual fund, the net asset value per share usually represents the fund's market price, subject to a possible sales or redemption charge. For a closed end fund, the market price may vary significantly from the net asset value.

NET INCOME

The company's total earnings, reflecting revenues adjusted for costs of doing business, depreciation, interest, taxes and other expenses.

NOISE

Price and volume fluctuations that can confuse interpretation of market direction.

NO LOAD MUTUAL FUND

An open-end investment company, shares of which are sold without a sales charge. There can be other distribution charges, however, such as Article 12b-1 fees. A true "no load" fund will have neither a sales charge nor a distribution fee.

OBJECTIVE (MUTUAL FUNDS)

The fund's investment strategy category as stated in the prospectus. There are more than 20 standardized categories.

OPENING PURCHASE

A transaction in which the purchaser's intention is to create or increase a long position in a given series of options.

OPENING SALE
A transaction in which the seller's intention is to create or increase a short position in a given series of options.

OPEN INTEREST
The number of outstanding option contracts in the exchange market or in a particular class or series.

OPTION
Gives the buyer the right, but not the obligation, to buy or sell stock at a set price on or before a given date. Investors, not companies, issue options. Investors who purchase call options bet the stock will be worth more than the price set by the option (the strike price), plus the price they paid for the option itself. Buyers of put options bet the stock's price will go down below the price set by the option.

OTHER CURRENT ASSETS
Value of non-cash assets, including prepaid expenses and accounts receivable, due within 1 year.

OTHER LONG TERM LIABILITIES
Value of leases, future employee benefits, deferred taxes and other obligations not requiring interest payments that must be paid over a period of more than 1 year.

OTHER SOURCES
Amount of funds generated during the period from operations by sources other than depreciation or deferred taxes. Part of Free Cash Flow calculation.

OUT OF THE MONEY
A call option is out-of-the-money if the strike price is greater than the market price of the underlying security. A put option is out-of-the-money if the strike price is less than the market price of the underlying security.

OVERBOUGHT\OVERSOLD INDICATOR
An indicator that attempts to define when prices have moved too far and too fast in either direction and thus are vulnerable to reaction.

PAYMENT DATE
Date on which a declared stock dividend or a bond interest payment is scheduled to be made.

PHONE SWITCHING

In mutual funds, the ability to transfer shares between funds in the same family by telephone request. There may be a charge associated with these transfers. Phone switching is also possible among different fund families if the funds are held in street name by a particpating broker/dealer.

PIVOT

Price level established as being significant by the market's failure to penetrate or as being significant when a sudden increase in volume accompanies the move through the price level.

POINT AND FIGURE CHART

A price-only chart that takes into account only whole integer changes in price, i.e., a 2-point change. Point and figure charting disregards the element of time and is solely used to record changes in price.

PREFERRED STOCK

A security that shows ownership in a corporation and gives the holder a claim, prior to the claim of common stockholders, on earnings and also generally on assets in the event of liquidation. Most preferred stock pays a fixed dividend, stated in a dollar amount or as a percentage of par value. This stock does not usually carry voting rights.

PREMIUM

The price of an option contract, determined on the exchange, which the buyer of the option pays to the option writer for the rights to the option contract.

PRICE/BOOK RATIO

Compares a stock's market value to the value of total assets less total liabilities (book). Determined by dividing current price by common stockholders' equity per share (book value), adjusted for stock splits. Also called Market-to-Book.

PRICE/EARNINGS RATIO

Shows the "multiple" of earnings at which a stock sells. Determined by dividing current price by current earnings per share (adjusted for stock splits). Earnings per share for the P/E ratio is determined by dividing earnings for past 12 months by the number of common shares outstanding. Higher "multiple" means investors have higher expectations for future growth, and have bid up the stock's price.

P/E RATIO EQUATION
Assume XYZ Co sells for $26.50 per share and has earned $2.65 per share this year

$26.50 = 10 times $2.65

XYZ stock sells for 10 times earnings.

PRICE/SALES RATIO
Determined by dividing stock's current price by revenue per share (adjusted for stock splits). Revenue per share for the P/S ratio is determined by dividing revenue for past 12 months by number of shares outstanding.

PRIMARY MARKET
The first buyer of a newly issued security buys that security in the primary market. All subsequent trading of those securities is done in the secondary market.

PROFIT MARGIN
Indicator of profitability. Determined by dividing net income by revenue for the same 12-month period. Result is shown as a percentage.

PROGRAM TRADING
Trades based on signals from computer programs, usually entered directly from the trader's computer to the market's computer system and executed automatically.

PROSPECTUS
Formal written document to sell securities that describes the plan for a proposed business enterprise, or the facts concerning an existing one, that an investor needs to make an informed decision. Prospectuses are used by Mutual Funds to describe the fund objectives, risks and other essential information.

PROXY
Document intended to provide shareholders with information necessary to vote in an informed manner on matters to be brought up at a stockholders' meeting. Includes information on closely held shares. Shareholders can and often do give management their proxy, representing the right and responsibility to vote their shares as specified in the proxy statement.

PUT OPTION
An option contract that gives the holder the right to sell (or "put"), and places upon the writer the obligation to purchase, a specified number of shares of the underlying stock at the given strike price on or before the expiration date of the contract.

QUICK RATIO

Indicator of a company's financial strength (or weakness). Calculated by taking current assets less inventories, divided by current liabilities. Also called Acid Test.

RANGE

The difference between the high and low price during a given period.

RETURN

The percentage gain or loss for a mutual fund in a specific time period. This number assumes that all distributions are reinvested.

RECORD DATE

Date by which a shareholder must officially own shares in order to be entitled to a dividend. For example, a firm might declare a dividend on Nov 1, payable Dec 1 to holders of record Nov 15. Once a trade is executed an investor becomes the "owner of record" on settlement, which currently takes 5 business days for securities, and one business day for mutual funds. Stocks trade ex-dividend the fourth day before the record date, since the seller will still be the owner of record and is thus entitled to the dividend.

REDEMPTION CHARGE

The commission charged by a mutual fund when redeeming shares. For example, a 2% redemption charge (also called a "back end load") on the sale of shares valued at $1000 will result in payment of $980 (or 98% of the value) to the investor. This charge may decrease or be eliminated as shares are held for longer time periods.

RELATIVE STRENGTH

A stock's price movement over the past year as compared to a market index (the S&P 500). Value below 1.0 means the stock shows relative weakness in price movement (underperformed the market); a value above 1.0 means the stock shows relative strength over the 1-year period. Equation for Relative Strength: [current stock price/year-ago stock price] [current S&P 500/year-ago S&P 500]

RETRACEMENT

A price movement in the opposite direction of the previous trend.

RETURN ON ASSETS (ROA)

Indicator of profitability. Determined by dividing net income for the past 12 months by total assets. Result is shown as a percentage.

RETURN ON EQUITY (ROE)
Indicator of profitability. Determined by dividing net income for the past 12 months by common stockholders' equity (adjusted for stock splits). Result is shown as a percentage.

REVERSE STOCK SPLIT
A proportionate decrease in the number of shares, but not the value of shares of stock held by shareholders. Shareholders maintain the same percentage of equity as before the split. For example, a 1-for-3 split would result in stockholders owning 1 share for every 3 shares owned before the split. A firm generally institutes a reverse split to boost its stock's market price and attract investors.

RIGHTS OFFERING
Issuance of "rights" to current shareholders allowing them to purchase additional shares, usually at a discount to market price. Shareholders who do not exercise these rights are usually diluted by the offering. Rights are often transferrable, allowing the holder to sell them on the open market to others who may wish to exercise them. Rights offerings are particularly common to closed end funds, which cannot otherwise issue additional common stock.

SALES CHARGE
The fee charged by a mutual fund when purchasing shares, usually payable as a commission to a marketing agent, such as a financial advisor, who is thus compensated for his assistance to a purchaser. It represents the difference, if any, between the share purchase price and the share net asset value.

SEC
The Securities and Exchange Commission, the primary federal regulatory agency of the securities industry.

SECONDARY MARKET
A market that provides for the purchase or sale of previously owned securities. Most trading is done in the secondary market. The New York Stock Exchange, as well as all other stock exchanges, the bond markets, etc., are secondary markets.

SELLING SHORT
If an investor thinks the price of a stock is going down, the investor could borrow the stock from a broker and sell it. Eventually, the investor must buy the stock back on the open market. For instance, you borrow 1000 shares of XYZ on July 1 and sell it for $8 per share. Then, on Aug 1, you purchase 1000 shares of XYZ at $7 per share. You've made $1000 (less commissions and other fees) by selling short.

SERIES

Options: All option contracts of the same class that also have the same unit of trade, expiration date, and exercise price. Stocks: shares which have common characteristics, such as rights to ownership and voting, dividends, par value, etc. In the case of many foreign shares, one series may be owned only by citizens of the country in which the stock is registered.

SETTLEMENT DATE

The date on which payment is made to settle a trade. For stocks traded on US exchanges, settlement is currently 5 business days after the trade, but this will be reduced to 3 days in 1995. For mutual funds, settlement usually occurs in the U.S. the day following the trade. In some regional markets, foreign shares may require months to settle.

SHARE REPURCHASE

Program by which a corporation buys back its own shares in the open market. It is usually done when shares are undervalued. Since it reduces the number of shares outstanding and thus increases earnings per share, it tends to elevate the market value of the remaining shares held by stockholders.

SHORT POSITION (OPTIONS)

A position wherein a person's interest in a particular series of options is as a net writer (i.e., the number of contracts sold exceeds the number of contracts bought).

SHORT POSITION (STOCKS)

Occurs when a person sells stocks she/he does not yet own. Shares must be borrowed, before the sale, to make "good delivery" to the buyer. Eventually, the shares must be bought to close out the transaction. Technique is used when an investor believes the stock price is going down.

SHORT SALE

Selling a security that the seller does not own but is committed to repurchasing eventually. It is used to capitalize on an expected decline in the security's price.

SLIPPAGE

The difference between estimated transaction costs and actual transaction costs. The difference is usually composed of revisions to price difference or spread and commission costs.

SIC

Abbreviation for Standard Industrial Classification. Each 4-digit code represents a unique business activity.

STOCK DIVIDEND

Payment of a corporate dividend in the form of stock rather than cash. The stock dividend may be additional shares in the company, or it may be shares in a subsidiary being spun off to shareholders. Stock dividends are often used to conserve cash needed to operate the business. Unlike a cash dividend, stock dividends are not taxed until sold.

STOP (-LOSS) ORDER

An order to sell a stock when the price falls to a specified level.

STRIKE PRICE

The stated price per share for which underlying stock may be purchased (in the case of a call) or sold (in the case of a put) by the option holder upon exercise of the option contract.

10-K

Annual report required by the SEC each year. Provides a comprehensive overview of a company's state of business. Must be filed within 90 days after fiscal year end. A 10Q report is filed quarterly.

TICK INDICATOR

A market indicator based on the number of stocks whose last trade was an uptick or a downtick. Used as an indicator of market sentiment or psychology to try to predict the market's trend.

TIME VALUE

The portion of the premium that is based on the amount of time remaining until the expiration date of the option contract, and that the underlying components that determine the value of the option may change during that time. Time value is generally equal to the difference between the premium and the intrinsic value.

TOTAL REVENUE

Total sales and other revenue for the period shown. Known as "turnover" in the UK.

TRADE

A verbal (or electronic) transaction involving one party buying a security from another party. Once a trade is consummated, it is considered "done" or final. Settlement occurs 1-5 business days later.

TRADE DATE

The date on which a trade occurs. Trades generally settle (are paid for) 1-5 business days after a trade date. With stocks, settlement is generally 5 business days after the trade.

TRADING RANGE

The difference between the high and low prices traded during a period of time; with commodities, the high/low price limit established by the exchange for a specific commodity for any one day's trading.

TURNOVER

Mutual Funds: a measure of trading activity during the previous year, expressed as a percentage of the average total assets of the fund. A turnover ratio of 25% means that the value of trades represented one-fourth of the assets of the fund. Finance: the number of times a given asset, such as inventory, is replaced during the accounting period, usually a year. Corporate: the ratio of annual sales to net worth, representing the extent to which a company can grow without outside capital. Markets: the volume of shares traded as a percent of total shares listed during a specified period, usually a day or a year. Great Britain: total revenue

12B-1 FEES

The percent of a mutual fund's assets used to defray marketing and distribution expenses. The amount of the fee is stated in the fund's prospectus. The SEC has recently proposed that 12b-1 fees in excess of 0.25% be classed as a load. A true "no load" fund has neither a sales charge nor 12b-1 fee.

TYPE The classification of an option contract as either a put or a call.

UNCOVERED CALL

A short call option position in which the writer does not own shares of underlying stock represented by his option contracts. Also called a "naked" call, it is much riskier for the writer than a covered call, where the writer owns the underlying stock. If the buyer of a call exercises the option to call, the writer would be forced to buy the stock at market price.

UNCOVERED PUT

A short put option position in which the writer does not have a corresponding short stock position or has not deposited, in a cash account, cash or cash equivalents equal to the exercise value of the put. Also called "naked" puts, the writer has pledged to buy the stock at a certain price if the buyer of the options chooses to exercise it. The nature of uncovered options means the writer's risk is unlimited.

UNDERLYING SECURITY
Options: the security subject to being purchased or sold upon exercise of an option contract. For example, IBM stock is the underlying security to IBM options. Depository receipts: the class, series and number of the foreign shares represented by the depository receipt.

VOLATILITY
A measure of risk based on standard deviation in fund performance over 3 years. Scale is 1-9; higher rating indicates higher risk.

Std Deviation	Rating	Std Deviation	Rating
up to 7.99	1	20.00-22.99	6
8.00-10.99	2	23.00-25.99	7
11.00-13.99	3	26.00-28.99	8
14.00-16.99	4	29.00 and up	9
17.00-19.99	5		

WALLFLOWER
Stock that has fallen out of favor with investors; tends to have a low P/E.

WANTED FOR CASH
A statement displayed on market tickers which indicates that a bidder will pay cash for same day settlement of a block of a specified security.

WARRANT
A security entitling the holder to buy a proportionate amount of stock at some specified future date at a specified price, usually one higher than current market. This "warrant" is then traded as a security, the price of which reflects the value of the underlying stock. Warrants are usually issued as a "sweetener" bundled with another class of security to enhance the marketability of the latter.

WASTING ASSET
An asset which has a limited life and thus, decreases in value (depreciates) over time. Also applied to consumed assets, such as gas, and termed "depletion."

WATCH LIST
A list of securities selected for special surveillance by a brokerage, exchange or regulatory organization; firms on the list are often takeover targets, companies planning to issue new securities or stocks showing unusual activity.

WITHDRAWAL PLAN
The ability to establish automatic periodic mutual fund redemptions and have proceeds mailed directly to the investor.

WRITER
The seller of an option contract.

YIELD
The percentage rate of return paid on a stock in the form of dividends, or the rate of interest paid on a bond or note.

YIELD TO CALL
The percentage rate of a bond or note, if you were to buy and hold the security until the call date. This yield is valid only if the security is called prior to maturity. Generally bonds are callable over several years and normally are called at a slight premium. The calculation of yield to call is based on the coupon rate, length of time to the call and the market price.

YIELD TO MATURITY
The percentage rate of return paid on a bond, note or other fixed income security if you buy and hold it to its maturity date. The calculation for YTM is based on the coupon rate, length of time to maturity and market price. It assumes that coupon interest paid over the life of the bond will be reinvested at the same rate.

NASDAQ 100 Stocks

COMPANY	SYMBOL	% OF INDEX MARKET VALUE
3Com Corporation	COMS	0.79
Adaptec, Inc.	ADPT	0.61
ADC Telecommunications, Inc.	ADCT	0.51
Adobe Systems Incorporated	ADBE	0.46
ADTRAN, Inc.	ADTN	0.17
Altera Corporation	ALTR	0.66
American Greetings Corporation	AGREA	0.34
American Power Conversion Corporation	APCC	0.27
Amgen Inc.	AMGN	2.42
Andrew Corporation	ANDW	0.36
Apple Computer, Inc.	AAPL	0.35
Applied Materials, Inc.	AMAT	1.44
Ascend Communications, Inc.	ASND	0.76
Atmel Corporation	ATML	0.35
Autodesk, Inc.	ADSK	0.23
Bed Bath & Beyond Inc.	BBBY	0.29
Biogen, Inc.	BGEN	0.37
Biomet, Inc.	BMET	0.28
BMC Software, Inc.	BMCS	0.67
Boston Chicken, Inc.	BOST	0.23
Cascade Communications Corp.	CSCC	0.39
Centocor, Inc.	CNTO	0.29
Chiron Corporation	CHIR	0.47
Cintas Corporation	CTAS	0.4
Cirrus Logic, Inc.	CRUS	0.09
Cisco Systems, Inc.	CSCO	5.06
Comcast Corporation	CMCSK	0.45
Compuware Corporation	CPWR	0.49
Concord EFS, Inc.	CEFT	0.17
Corporate Express, Inc.	CEXP	0.18
Costco Companies Inc.	COST	0.91
Cracker Barrel Old Country Store, Inc.	CBRL	0.25
Dell Computer Corporation	DELL	2.26
DSC Communications Corporation	DIGI	0.36
Electronic Arts Inc.	ERTS	0.18
Electronics for Imaging, Inc.	EFII	0.3
Fastenal Company	FAST	0.23
Fiserv, Inc.	FISV	0.27
Food Lion, Inc.	FDLNB	0.25
FORE Systems, Inc.	FORE	0.16
Fort Howard Corporation	FORT	0.38
Gartner Group, Inc.	GART	0.32
Gateway 2000, Inc.	GATE	0.7
General Nutrition Companies, Inc.	GNCI	0.26
Genzyme Corporation	GENZ	0.25
Glenayre Technologies, Inc.	GEMS	0.09
HBO & Company	HBOC	0.75
HealthCare COMPARE Corp.	HCCC	0.22
IDEXX Laboratories, Inc.	IDXX	0.06
Informix Corporation	IFMX	0.16
Intel Corporation	INTC	19.04
Intuit Inc.	INTU	0.16
KLA Instruments Corporation	KLAC	0.35

Komag, Incorporated	KMAG	0.22
Linear Technology Corporation	LLTC	0.56
Maxim Integrated Products, Inc.	MXIM	0.5
McAfee Associates, Inc.	MCAF	0.37
McCormick & Company, Incorporated	MCCRK	0.24
MCI Communications Corporation	MCIC	3.28
Micron Electronics, Inc.	MUEI	0.3
Microsoft Corporation	MSFT	21.65
Molex Incorporated	MOLX	0.36
Nextel Communications, Inc.	NXTL	0.44
Nordstrom, Inc.	NOBE	0.47
Northwest Airlines Corporation	NWAC	0.57
Novell, Inc.	NOVL	0.41
Oracle Corporation	ORCL	4.11
Outback Steakhouse, Inc.	OSSI	0.13
Oxford Health Plans, Inc.	OXHP	0.73
PACCAR Inc	PCAR	0.45
PacifiCare Health Systems, Inc.	PHSYB	0.32
Paging Network, Inc.	PAGE	0.1
PairGain Technologies, Inc.	PAIR	0.23
Parametric Technology Corporation	PMTC	0.88
Paychex, Inc.	PAYX	0.47
PeopleSoft, Inc.	PSFT	0.67
PETsMART, Inc.	PETM	0.27
PhyCor, Inc.	PHYC	0.21
QUALCOMM Incorporated	QCOM	0.45
Quantum Corporation	QNTM	0.38
Quintiles Transnational Corp.	QTRN	0.26
Republic Industries, Inc.	RWIN	1.1
RPM, Inc.	RPOW	0.19
Sigma-Aldrich Corporation	SIAL	0.44
Staples, Inc.	SPLS	0.47
Starbucks Corporation	SBUX	0.34
Stryker Corporation	STRY	0.45
Sun Microsystems, Inc.	SUNW	1.63
SunGard Data Systems, Inc.	SNDT	0.29
Sybase, Inc.	SYBS	0.19
Synopsys, Inc.	SNPS	0.18
Tele-Communications, Inc.	TCOMA	1.11
Tellabs, Inc.	TLAB	1.14
Tyson Foods, Inc.	TYSNA	0.35
U.S. Robotics Corporation	USRX	0.68
Viking Office Products, Inc.	VKNG	0.19
Wisconsin Central Transportation Corporation	WCLX	0.28
WorldCom, Inc.	WCOM	3.12
Worthington Industries,		

Price Codes & Commodity Symbols

EXPIRATION MONTH SYMBOLS

DELIVERY MONTH	COMMODITIES	OPTIONS CALL	OPTIONS PUT	DELIVERY MONTH	COMMODITIES OPTIONS CALL	COMMODITIES OPTIONS PUT
January	F	A	M	July	N	G	S
February	G	B	N	August	Q	H	T
March	H	C	O	September	U	I	U
April	J	D	P	October	V	J	V
May	K	E	Q	November	X	K	W
June	M	F	R	December	Z	L	X

OPTION STRIKE PRICE SYMBOLS

PRICE					CODE	/	PRICE					CODE	/	PRICE					CODE
5	105	205	305	405	A	/	40	140	240	340	440	H	/	75	175	275	375	475	O
10	110	210	310	410	B	/	45	145	245	345	445	I	/	80	180	280	380	480	P
15	115	215	315	415	C	/	50	150	250	350	450	J	/	85	185	285	385	485	Q
20	120	220	320	420	D	/	55	155	255	355	455	K	/	90	190	290	390	490	R
25	125	225	325	425	E	/	60	160	260	360	460	L	/	95	195	295	395	495	S
30	130	230	330	430	F	/	65	165	265	365	465	M	/	100	200	300	400	500	T
35	135	235	335	435	G	/	70	170	270	370	470	N	/	Non Standard Prices = U-Z					

Dow Index Stocks

DOW INDUSTRIAL INDEX COMPONENTS

AT&T	T	
Aluminum Co. of America	AA	
Allied-Signal Inc.	ALD	
American Express Co.	AXP	
Boeing Co.	BA	
Caterpillar Inc.	CAT	
Chevron Corp.	CHV	
Coca Cola Co.	KO	
Disney Co.	DIS	
Dupont	DD	
Eastman Kodak Co.	EK	
Exxon Corp.	XON	
General Electric Co.	GE	
General Motors	GM	
Goodyear Tire & Rubber		GT
Hewlett Packard		HWP
IBM	IBM	
International Paper Co.	IP	
Johnson & Johnson	JNJ	
JP Morgan		JPM
McDonalds		MCD
Merck & Co.	MRK	
Minnesota Mining & Manufacturing	MMM	
Philip Morris	MO	
Procter & Gamble Co.	PG	
Sears, Roebuck & Co.	S	
Travelers		TRV
Union Carbide Corp.	UK	
United Technologies	UTX	
Wal-Mart	WMT	

DOW TRANSPORTATION INDEX COMPONENTS

AMR Corp.		AMR
Airborne Freight Corp.		ABF
APL Ltd.	APL	
Alaska Air	ALK	
Burlington Northern Inc.	BNI	
CNF Transp		
CSX Corp.		CSX
Caliber Systems Inc.	CBB	
ConRail	CRR	
Delta Air Lines Inc.	DAL	
Federal Express Corp.		FDX
Ill. Central	IC	
Norfolk Southern Corp.		NSC
Ryder System Inc.	R	
Southwest Airlines Co.		LUV

UAL Corp.	UAL
Union Pacific Corp.	UNP
USAir Group Inc.	U
XTRA Corp.	XTR
Yellow Corp.	YELL

DOW UTILITY INDEX COMPONENTS

American Electric Power Co.	AEP
Centerior Energy Corp.	CX
Consolidated Edison Co. of New York	ED
Consolidated Natural Gas Co.	CNG
DTE Energy	DTE
Edison Intl.	EIX
Houston Industries Inc.	HOU
Niagara Mohawk Power Corp.	NMK
Noram Energy	NAE
Pacific Gas & Electric Co.	PCG
PanEnergy	PEL
Peco	PE
Peoples Energy Corp.	PGL
Public Service Enterprise Group	PEG
Unicom Corp.	UMCP

NOTE: THIS LIST CURRENT AS OF APRIL 1997.

Futures Contract Information - CME

Chicago Mercantile Exchange (CME)

Contract	Symbol	Delivery Months	Trading Hours	Size	Minimum Tick	Daily Limit
Australian Dollar	AD	H,M,U,Z	7:20am - 2:00pm; Globex 2:30pm - 6:50am+	AD100,000	.01¢/AD = $10.00	Opening Limit 400 pts. = $4,000*
Brazilian Real	BR	H,M,U,Z	7:20am - 2:00pm; Globex 2:30pm - 6:50am+	BR100,000	.01¢/BR = $10.00	Consult Exchange
British Pound	BP	H,M,U,Z	7:20am - 2:00pm; Globex 2:30pm - 6:50am+	BP62,500	.02¢/BP = $12.50	Opening Limit 800pts. = $5,000*
British Pound Rolling Spot	RP	H,M,U,Z (X=Daily Adj.)	7:00am - 2:00pm; Globex 2:30pm - 6:50am+	BP250,000	.0001 = $25.00	Consult Exchange
Canadian Dollar	CD	H,M,U,Z	7:20am - 2:00pm; Globex 2:30pm - 6:50am+	CD100,000	.01¢/CD = $10.00	Opening Limit 400 pts. = $4,000*
Deutsche Mark	DM	H,M,U,Z	7:20am - 2:00pm; Globex 2:30pm - 6:50am+	DM125,000	.01¢/DM = $12.50	Opening Limit 400 pts. = %5,000*
Deutsche Mark Forward	FM, WM for swaps	All Months	7:00am - 2:00pm; Globex 2:30pm - 6:50am+	US$250,000	.000025 = DM6.25	Consult Exchange
Deutsche Mark Rolling Spot	RD	H,M,U,Z (X=Daily Adj.)	7:00am - 2:00pm; Globex 2:30pm - 6:50am+	US$250,000	.0001 = $25.00	Consult Exchange
DeutscheMark/Yen	DJ	H,M,U,Z	7:20am - 2:00pm; Globex 2:30pm - 6:50am+	JY per DM	.01 = JY1,250	Consult Exchange
Eurodollars	ED	H,M,U,Z	7:20am - 2:00pm; Globex 2:45pm - 6:50am+	$1,000,000	.01 = $25.00	None (Globex)
Euromark	EK	H,M,U,Z	7:20am - 2:00pm	DM1,000,000	.01 = DM25.00	None
Fed. Funds Rate	NA	All Months	7:20am - 2:00pm; Globex 2:45pm - 6:50am+	$3,000,000	.005 = $12.50	None
Feeder Cattle	FC	F,H,J,K,Q,U,V,X	9:05am - 1:00pm	50,000 lbs.	2.5¢/cwt. = $12.50	1.5¢/lb. = $750
Fluid Milk	DA	G,J,M,N,U,X	8:00am = 1:00pm	50,000 lbs.	2.5¢/cwt. = $12.50	1.5¢/lb. = $750
French Franc	FR	H,M,U,Z	7:20am - 2:00pm; Globex 2:30pm - 6:50am+	FF500,000	.002/FF = $10.00	Opening Limit 500 pts. = $2,500*
FT-SE 100 Index	FI	H,M,U,Z	8:30am - 3:15pm	$50 x Index	.5 = $25.00	None
GSCI	GI	G,J,M,Q,VZ	8:15am - 2:15pm; GLOBEX 2:45pm - 8:00pm+	$250 x Index	.10 = $25.00	None (Globex = 30 pts.)
Japanese Yen	JY	H,M,U,Z	7:20am - 2:00pm; Globex 2:30pm - 6:50am+	JY12,500,000	.0001¢/JY = $12.50	Opening Limit 400 pts. = $5,000*
Japanese Yen Rolling Spot	RY	H,M,U,Z	7:00am - 2:00pm; Globex 2:30pm - 6:50am+	US$250,000	.0001 = ¥2,500,000	Consult Exchange
Japanese Yen Forward	F	All Months	7:00am - 2:00pm; Globex 2:30pm - 6:50am+	US$250,000	.000025 = JY625.00	Consult Exchange
Lean Hogs	LN	G,J,M,Q,VZ	9:10am - 1:00pm	40,000 lbs.	2.5¢/cwt. = $10.00	1.5¢/lb. = $600
LIBOR	EM	All Months	7:20am - 2:00pm; Globex 2:45pm - 6:50am+	$3,000,000	.01 = $25.00	None (Globex = 200 pts.)
Live Cattle	LC	G,J,M,Q,VZ	9:05am - 1:00pm	40,000 lbs.	2.5¢/cwt. = $10.00	1.5¢/lb. = $600
Live Hogs	LH	G,J,M,N,Q,VZ	9:10am - 1:00pm	40,000 lbs.	2.5¢/cwt. = $10.00	1.5¢/lb. = $600
MMI	MM	All Months	8:15am - 3:15pm; Globex 3:45pm - 8:00pm+	$500 x Index	.05 = $25.00	Consult Exchange
Mexican Peso	ME	H,M,U,Z	8:20am - 2:00pm; Globex 2:30pm - 6:50am+	MP500,000	.0025¢/MP = $12.50	Consult Exchange
Nikkei	225NK		8:00am - 3:15pm	$5 x Average	5 pts. = $25.00	Consult Exchange
Pork Bellies	PB	G,H,K,N,Q	9:10am - 1:00pm	40,000 lbs.	2.5$/cwt. = $10.00	3¢/lb. = $1,200
Random Length Lumber	LB	F,H,K,N,U,X	9:00am - 1:05pm	80,000 bd ft.	10¢/100 bd ft. = $8.00	Consult Exchange
Russell 2000	RL	H,M,U,Z	8:30am - 3:15pm; Globex 3:45pm - 8:00pm+	$500 x Index	.05 = $25.00	Consult exchange
S&P 500	SP	H,M,U,Z	8:30am - 3:15pm; Globex 3:45pm - 8:00pm+	$500 x Index	.05 = $25.00	Consult Exchange
S&P MidCap 400	MD	H,M,U,Z	8:30am - 3:15pm; Globex 3:45pm - 8:00pm+	$500 x Index	.05 = $25.00	Consult Exchange
Swiss Franc	SF	H,M,U,Z	7:20am - 2:00pm; Globex 2:30pm - 6:50am+	SF125,000	.01¢/SF = $12.50	Opening Limit 400 pts. = $5,000*
U.S. T-Bill	TB	H,M,U,Z	7:20am - 2:00pm; Globex 2:45pm - 6:50am+	$1,000,000	.01 = $25.00	None (Globex = 200 pts.)
U.S. T-Bills 1yr.	YR	H,M,U,Z	7:20am - 2:00pm; Globex 2:45pm - 6:50am+	$500,000	.005 = $25.00	None (Globex = 200 pts.)

Futures Contract Information - CBOT

Chicago Board of Trade (CBOT)

Contract	Symbol	Delivery Months	Trading Hours	Size	Minimum Tick	Daily Limit
Anhydrous Ammonia	NZ	G,J,M,U,Z	9:05am - 12:20pm	100 tons	10¢/ton = $10.00	$10/ton = $1,000*
Can. T-Bonds 10 Yr.	CN	H,M,U,Z	7:20am - 2:00pm; P,A+	CD100,000	1/100 = $10.00	3 pts. = $3,000*
Corn	C	H,K,N,U,Z	9:30am - 1:15pm	5,000 bu.	1/4¢bu. = $12.50	12¢/bu. = $600*
U.S. Corn Yld. Ins.	YC	U,V,X,F	10:30am - 12:45pm	$100 x Yld. Est.	1/10bu./acre = $10.00	15¢/bu. = $1,500
Diammon. Phosphate	FZ	H,M,U,Z	9:00am - 12:15pm	100 tons	10¢/ton = $10.00	$10/ton = $1,000*
Gold (Kilo)	KI	G,J,M,Q,V,Z	7:20am - 1:40pm	1 kilo	10¢/oz. = $3.22	$50/oz. = $1,607.50*
Gold	GH	G,J,M,Q,V,Z	7:20am - 1:40pm; 5:20pm - 8:05pm+	100 troy oz.	10¢/oz. = $10.00	$50/oz. = $5,000*
Muni Bond Index	MB	H,M,U,Z	7:20am - 2:00pm; P,A+	1,000 x Index	1/32 = $31.25	3 pts. = $3,000*
Oats	O	H,K,N,U,Z	9:30am - 1:15pm	5,000 bu.	1/4¢bu. = $12.50	10¢/bu. = $500*
Rough Rice	RR	F,H,K,N,U,X	9:15am - 1:15pm	2,000 cwl.	5¢/cwt. = $10.00	30¢/cwt. = $600*
Silver	AG	G,J,M,Q,V,Z	7:25am - 1:25pm	1,000 troy oz.	.1¢/oz. - $1.00	$1/oz. = $1,000*
Silver	SV	G,J,M,Q,V,Z	7:25am - 1:25pm; 5:20pm - 8:05pm+	5,000 troy oz.	.1¢/oz. - $5.00	$1/oz. - $5,000*
Soybeans	S	F,H,K,N,Q,U,X	9:30am - 1:15pm	5,000 bu.	1/4¢bu. = $12.50	30¢/bu. = $1,500*
Soybean Meal	SM	F,H,K,N,Q,U,V,Z	9:30am - 1:15pm	100 tons	10¢/ton = $10.00	$10/ton = $1,000*
Soybean Oil	BO	F,H,K,N,Q,U,V,Z	9:30am - 1:15pm	60,000 lbs.	.01¢/lb. = $6.00	1¢/lb. = $600*
30 day Fed. Funds	FF	All Months	7:20am - 2:00pm; P,A+	$5,000,000	.01 = $41.67++	150 pts. = $6,250.50*
U.S. T-Bonds	US	H,M,U,Z	7:20am - 2:00pm; 5:20pm - 8:05pm; P,A+	$100,000	1/32 = $31.25	3 pts. = $3,000*
U.S. T-Notes 10 yr.	TY	H,M,U,Z	7:20am - 2:00pm; 5:20pm - 8:05pm; P,A+	$100,000	1/32 = $31.25	3 pts. = $3,000*
U.S. T-Notes 2 yr.	TU	H,M,U,Z	7:20am - 2:00pm; 5:20pm - 8:05pm; P,A+	$200,000	1/128 = $15.625	1 pt. = $2,000*
U.S. T-Notes 5 yr.	FV	H,M,U,Z	7:20am - 2:00pm; 5:20pm - 8:05pm; P,A+	$100,000	1/64 = $15.625	3 pts. = $3,000*
Wheat	W	H,K,N,U,Z	9:30am - 1:15pm	5,000 bu.	1/4¢bu. = $12.50	20¢/bu. = $1,000*

Futures Contract Information - MIDAM

Mid America Exchange (MACE)

Contract	Symbol	Delivery Months	Trading Hours	Size	Minimum Tick	Daily Limit
Australian Dollar	XA	H,M,U,Z	7:20am - 2:15pm	AD50,000	.01¢/AD = $5.00	None
British Pound	XP	H,M,U,Z	7:20am - 2:15pm	BP12,500	.02¢/BP = $2.50	None
Canadian Dollar	XD	H,M,U,Z	7:20am - 2:15pm	CD50,000	.01¢/CD = $5.00	None
Corn	XC	H,K,N,U,Z	9:30am - 1:45pm	1,000 bu.	1/8¢/bu. = $1.25	12¢/bu. = $120*
Deutsche Mark	XM	H,M,U,Z	7:20am - 2:15pm	DM62,500	.01¢/DM = $6.25	None
Eurodollar	UD	H,M,U,Z	7:20am - 2:15pm	$500,000	.01 = $12.50	None
Japanese Yen	XJ	H,M,U,Z	7:20am - 2:15pm	JY6,250,000	.01¢/JY = $6.25	None
Live Cattle	XL	G,J,M,Q,V,Z	9:05am - 2:15pm	20,000 lbs.	.025¢/lb. = $5.00	1.5¢/lb. = $300
Live Hogs	XH	G,J,M,N,Q,V,Z	9:05am - 2:15pm	20,000 lbs.	.025¢/lb. = $5.00	1.5¢/lb. = $300
Gold	XK	All Months	7:20am - 2:40pm	33.2 troy oz.	10¢/oz. = $3.32	None
Oats	XO	H,K,N,U,Z	9:30am - 1:45pm	1,000 bu.	1/8¢/bu. = $1.25	10¢/bu. - $100*
Platinum	XU	F,J,N,V	7:10am - 1:40pm	25 troy oz.	10¢/oz. = $2.50	$25/oz. = $625
Silver	XY	All Months	7:25am - 1:40pm	1,000 tr. oz.	.1¢/oz. = $1.00	None
Soybeans	XS	F,H,K,N,Q,U,X	9:30am - 1:45pm	1,000 bu.	1/8¢/bu. = $1.25	30¢/bu. = $300*
Soybean Meal	XE	F,H,K,N,Q,U,V,Z	9:30am - 1:45pm	50 tons	10¢/ton = $5.00	$10/ton = $500*
Soybean Oil	XX	F,H,K,N,Q,U,V,Z	9:30am - 1:45pm	30,000 lbs.	.01¢/lb. = $3.00	1¢/lb. = $300
Swiss Franc	XF	H,M,U,Z	7:20am - 2:15pm	SF62,500	.01¢/SF = $6.25	None
U.S. T-Bills	XT	H,M,U,Z	7:20am - 2:15pm	$500,000	.01 = $12.50	None
U.S. T-Bonds	XB	H,M,U,Z	7:20am - 3:15pm	$50,000	1/32 = $15.62	3 pts. = $1,500
U.S. T-Notes 10 yr.	XN	H,M,U,Z	7:20am - 3:15pm	$50,000	1/32 = $15.62	3 pts. = $1,500*
U.S. T-Notes 5 yr.	XX	H,M,U,Z	7:20am - 3:15pm	$50,000	1/64 = $7.81	3 pts. = $1,500*
Wheat	XW	H,K,N,U,Z	9:30am - 1:45pm	1,000 bu.	1/8¢/bu. = $1.25	20¢/bu. = $200

Order Types Accepted by Exchanges

Exchange	Limit	Market	MOC	Fill Or Kill	Stop	Stop Limit	SWL	SCO	SLCO	MIT	OCO
CME											
All Markets	Yes	Yes	Yes	Yes	Yes	Yes	Yes	Yes	Yes*	Yes	Yes
CBOT											
All Markets	Yes	Yes	Yes	Yes	Yes	No	No	No	No	No	No
COMEX											
All Markets	Yes	Yes	Yes	Yes	Yes	Yes	Yes	Yes	No	Yes	MOC
NYMEX											
All Markets	Yes	Yes	Yes	Yes	Yes	Yes	Yes	Yes	No	Yes	Yes
NYCE											
Cotton	Yes	Yes	Yes	Yes	Yes	Yes*	Yes	Yes	No	Yes	Yes*
Orange Juice	Yes	Yes	Yes	Yes	Yes	Yes	Yes	Yes	No	Yes*	Yes*
Dollar Index	Yes	Yes	Yes	Yes	Yes	Yes	Yes	Yes*	No	Yes	Yes*
CSCE											
Coffee	Yes	Yes	Yes	Yes	Yes	Yes	Yes	Yes	No	Yes	Yes*
Sugar	Yes	Yes	Yes	Yes	Yes	Yes	Yes	Yes	No	Yes	Yes
Cocoa	Yes	Yes	Yes	Yes	Yes	Yes	Yes	Yes	No	Yes	Yes
NYFE											
All Markets	Yes	Yes	Yes	Yes	Yes	Yes	Yes	Yes	No	Yes	MOC
KCBT											
Value Line	Yes	Yes	Yes	Yes	Yes	Yes	Yes*	Yes	Yes	Yes	Yes
Wheat	Yes	Yes	Yes	Yes	Yes	Yes	Yes*	Yes	Yes	Yes	Yes
MID-AM											
All Markets	Yes	Yes	Yes	Yes	Yes	No	No	Yes	No	No	Yes**

SWL=Stop With Limit
SCO=Stop Close Only
MOC=Market On Close
SLCO=Stop Limit Close Only
MIT=Market If Touched
OCO=Order Cancels Order

*=Not Held   **=No Meats

Resources On The Internet

Economic Data

http://woodrow.mpls.frb.fed.us Federal Reserve Bank of Minneapolis

http://www.stls.frb.org   Federal Reserve Bank of St. Louis

http://www.bankamerica.com   Bank of America

http://www.whitehouse.gov/fsbr/esbr.htm   Economic Briefing Room

http://www.usatoday.com/money/economy/econ0001.htm

       US Economic Indicators - USA Today

http://www.mexi.com/ECO/index.htm   Economic Charts

Charts & Quotes

http://www.dbc.com   Data Broadcasting Online

http://www.stockmaster.com   The Stockmaster

http://quote.yahoo.com   Yahoo Quotes

http://www.quote.com   QuoteCom

http://www.tfc-charts.w2d.com   TFC Commodity and Index Charts

http://networth.galt.com   Networth Galt

Financial News

http://djin.com   Dow Jones Investor Network (Audio)

http://www.bloomberg.com   Bloomberg Personal

http://metro.turnpike.net/holt/index.html The Holt Financial Report

http://www.ft.com   The Financial Times

http://www.barrons.com   Barron's Online

Exchanges

http://www.nyse.com   The New York Stock Exchange

http://www.csce.com   Coffee, Sugar & Cocoa Exchange

http://www.nymex.com   New York Mercantile Exchange

http://www.mgex.com   Minneapolis Grain Exchange

http://www.midam.com   The MIDAM Exchange

http://www.kcbt.com   Kansas City Board Of Trade

http://www.cboe.com   Chicago Board Options Exchange

http://www.cbt.com   Chicago Board of Trade

http://www.amex.com   The American Stock Exchange

http://www.libertynet.org/~phlx   The Philadelphia Stock Exchange

http://www.cme.com   The Chicago Mercantile Exchange

http://www.nasdaq.com   NASDAQ

Other Resources

http://centrex.com   Investor's Galleria

http://www.equis.com   Equis - Metastock

http://www.edgar-online.com   SEC Edgar Corporate Filings

http://www.omegaresearch.com   Omega - Tradestation

http://prophetdata.com   Prophet Information Systems

http://www.futuresmag.com   Futures Magazine

http://www.telenium.com   Candadian Quotes, News & Analyis

http://www.lombard.com   Lombard Brokerage

http://www.jackcarl.com   Jack Carl Commodity Brokerage

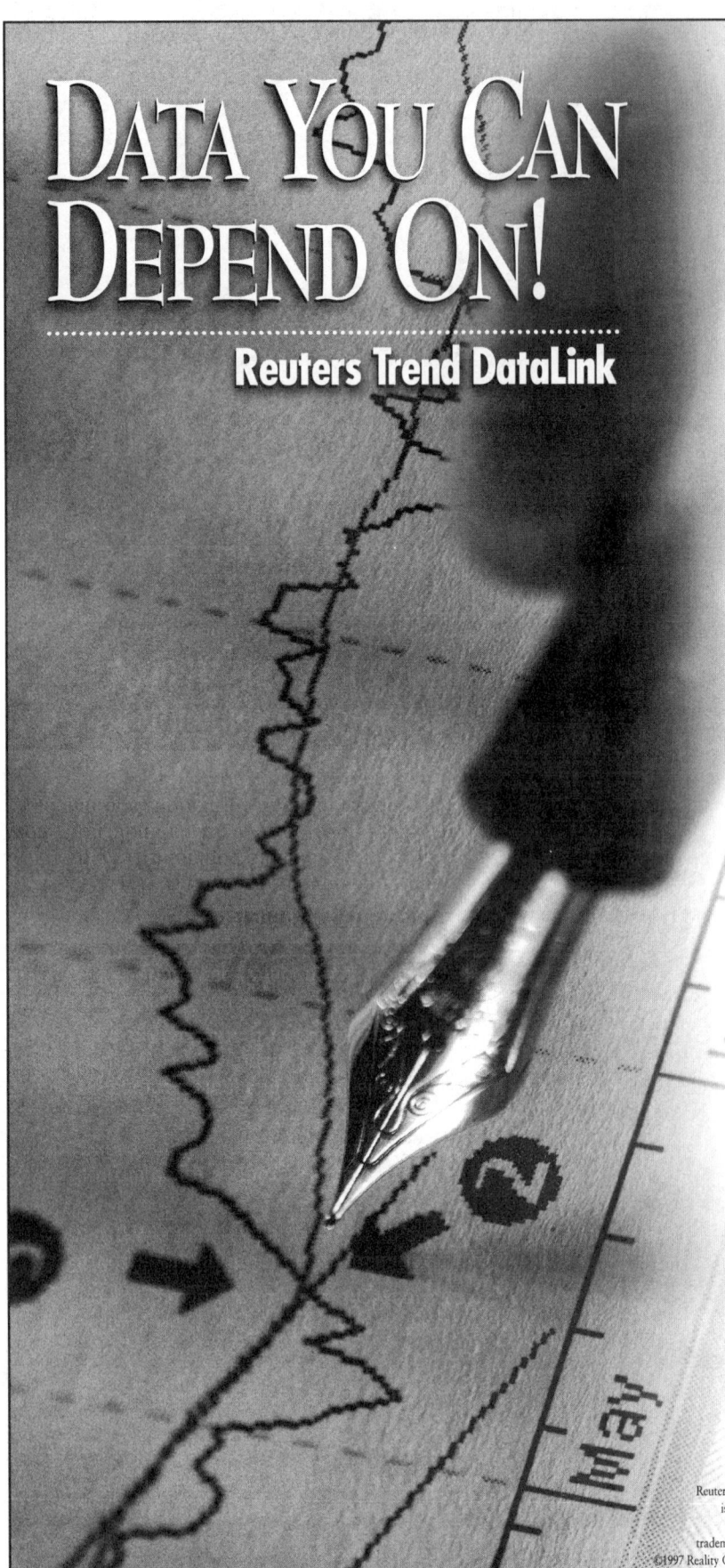

DATA YOU CAN DEPEND ON!

Reuters Trend DataLink

Reuters Trend DataLink™ (RTD) gives you access to the most accurate, comprehensive and dependable end-of-day price data available, whenever you need it.

Reliable Data

Reuters Trend DataLink's historical pricing database is maintained by more than 400 highly trained Reuters employees worldwide to ensure the accuracy of the data, so you don't need to worry.

Automatic Error Correction

Because the exchanges don't always report the data perfectly the first time, there's even an auto-correction feature that will correct any errors in the data that you've already stored. RTD is the *only* data service that provides completely effortless auto-correction.

Complete Market Coverage

With data on thousands of securities, Reuters Trend DataLink provides the most extensive collection available of historical pricing on equities, futures, commodities, indices, market indicators, and mutual funds. RTD's thorough coverage means you can be sure to find all the information you need.

Data on Demand

Reuters Trend DataLink is engineered to give you lightning-fast downloads, whether you are following ten contracts or ten thousand stocks. RTD is available via modem and through your Internet connection or the CompuServe network, 24-hours a day, 365-days a year; so you can access data at your convenience, not ours.

MetaStock-Compatible Data

Using RTD data is simple, as Reuters Trend DataLink works with The DownLoader™, the award winning data collection software from Equis International. You can use RTD data with MetaStock® or other MetaStock-compatible software to track, monitor, and technically analyze critical trends with indicators and studies to ultimately increase your profits.

Start collecting quotes today

Sign up now for Reuters Trend DataLink and give yourself the highest quality data available for your end-of-day investment analysis. Flexible online membership plans start at $22.45 per month.

Automate Your Investment Analysis

Your #1 Source for Finance & Investment Software!

Investors are always on the lookout for ways to increase their investment returns. At Anderson Investor's Software, Inc. we provide the software, data, and expertise to guide you to greater returns.

What is an Investor?

Everyone invests their valuable time and money everyday into a business venture of some kind. Whether this business is yours or somebody else's, we all make investments that we want to profit from. So why not use the best technology you can find to increase your returns! But, where do you look, which product do you buy, and is it right for you? That's why we put together this catalog. We wanted to provide a single source of financial products so that no matter what you are investing in, you have the best technology for the job.

The Mail-Order Catalog

Our mail-order catalog is packed with software to simplify investors' finances, make winning stock selections, and teach investors about the market.

http://www.INVEST-SOFT.com

Now you can shop on-line using our Internet catalog. Go to our web site at www.INVEST-SOFT.com

Catalog Topics

If you're looking to maximize the returns on your hard-earned money, then give us a call. We have software, CD-ROMs, books and service providers that allow you to use your computer to analyze investments, package loans for others, manage real estate, prepare your own Initial Public Offerings (IPOs), Employee Stock Ownership Plans (ESOPs), calculate loan schedules, manage your finances and more.

Raise Capital to Expand Any Business

Professional loan brokers and consultants use the products in our catalog to evaluate business ventures and real estate proposals, prepare loan packages, write business plans, or manage their money.

Call for a FREE 36-page Color Catalog Today!

CALL us toll free at 1-800-286-4106 and ask for a FREE Investor's Software Catalog. You will be glad to find the right technology for locating, making, or using money.

ANDERSON
INVESTOR's
Software, Inc.
INFO   314-918-0990
FAX   314-918-0980
SALES   800-286-4106

Internet http://www.invest-soft.com

FREE INVESTOR'S CATALOG

Your #1 Source for Finance & Investment Software

ANDERSON
INVESTOR's
Software, Inc.
800-286-4106

INFORMATION 314-918-0990
FAX 314-918-0980

30-day Money back guarantee. Prices subject to change

6-YRS HISTORIC STOCK DATA CD-ROM $49
Daily Open, High, Low, Close and Volume data on close to 9,000 stocks from the NYSE, AMEX and OTC exchanges. **Plus,** the DJIA & DJTA since 1897, DJBA since 1923, DJUA since 1934 and S&P 500 since 1928. **Plus,** 6-yrs of daily data on over 1,000 mutual funds along with a **FREE 30-day trial** to Investors FastTrack.

TELESCAN INVESTORS PLATFORM $199
Now you can combine all the vital tools and data you need all under windows to create the most powerful invvestment software available. You can create custom searches on a database of more than 14,000 issues using 250 industry groups. Screen for high growth stocks, perform "backtesting" to see how your searches performed historically, and search fundamental criteria for: EPS, Group Relative strength, Dividend and more.

METASTOCK & FULL DOWNLOADER $349
Purchase the leading technical analysis software package complete with a FULL downloader to 7 data providers, a historical data CD-ROM, a FREE trial to Reutor's Money Network, plus a FREE copy of the book "Technical Analysis from A to Z". Now you're ready to scan he markets for hot new issues, chart any symbol with built in drawing tools, and "backtest" your own trading systems to determine their profitability.

OMNITRADER Buy/Sell Signal Generator STOCKS $299 or Stocks & Futures $499

Backed by a decade of research into technical methods, OmniTrader tests and optimizes over 120 different technical analysis trading systems to produce highly confirmed buy & sell signals that maximize your liklihood for successful trades.

INVESTMENT ANALYSIS for Windows

AIQ *Trading Expert*.........................Yours for	**$695**
OmniTrader Stocks & Futures Signal Generator	**$499**
MetaStock w/Full Downloader & 5-yrs data CD	**$349**
TELESCAN Professional **PLATFORM**	**$299**
Windows On Wall Street Professional Investor	**$295**
OmniTrader Stocks Signal Generator	**$299**
Use **Monocle** for Mutual Fund Analysis	**$249**
SuperCharts 3.0 w/25-yrs stock data	**$199**
SMARTRADER w/historical stock CD-ROM	**$199**
TELESCAN INVESTORS PLATFORM (TIP)	**$179**
Windows On Wall Street Deluxe Investor	**$129**
Wall Street Investor Portfolio Mgmt/Analysis	**$129**
Learn with **Options Laboratory** Now	**$89**
Gain **FINANCIAL COMPETENCE**	**$89**
Wall Street Analyst Deluxe w/25-yrs data	**$59**
Windows On Wall Street Persoanl Investor	**$49**
Learn the **INVESTMENT BASICS**	**$49**

REAL ESTATE ANALYSIS & MGMT

Real Estate Investment Analysis	**$395**
Development Project Cost Analysis	**$149**
Keep your project ON SCHEDULE	**$195**
Tenant Pro Property Management	**$395**
EZ UNITS Property Management	**$99**
TValue for financial calculations	**$99**
Real Estate Lawyer	**$89**

HOT CD-ROM TITLES

Multimedia **Venture Capital** *Database*	**$195**
Instant Investor Stock, Econ. & comm. data	**$39**
Government Giveaways for Entrepreneurs	**$49**
Guide to Raising Money	**$29**
1000 Essential Business Forms & Letters	**$29**
6 Years stock data **CD-ROM**	**$49**
25 Years FUTURES data **CD-ROM**	**$129**

TRADERS PRESS, INC.®

INCORPORATED

P.O. BOX 6206
GREENVILLE, S.C. 29606

Books and Gifts
for Investors and Traders

Publishers of:

Commodity Spreads: A Historical Chart Perspective (Dobson)
The Trading Rule That Can Make You Rich* (Dobson)
Viewpoints of a Commodity Trader (Longstreet)
Commodities: A Chart Anthology (Dobson)
Profitable Grain Trading (Ainsworth)
A Complete Guide to Trading Profits (Paris)
Traders Guide to Technical Analysis (Hardy)
The Professional Commodity Trader (Kroll)
Jesse Livermore: Speculator-King (Sarnoff)
Understanding Fibonacci Numbers (Dobson)
Wall Street Ventures & Adventures through Forty Years (Wyckoff)
Winning Market Systems (Appel)
How to Trade in Stocks (Livermore)
Stock Market Trading Systems (Appel & Hitschler)
Study Helps in Point and Figure Technique (Wheelan)
Commodity Spreads: Analysis, Selection and Trading Techniques (Smith)
Comparison of Twelve Technical Trading Systems (Lukac, Brorsen, & Irwin)
Day Trading with Short Term Price Patterns and Opening Range Breakout (Crabel)
Understanding Bollinger Bands (Dobson)
Chart Reading for Professional Traders (Jenkins)
Geometry of Stock Market Profits (Jenkins)

Please write or call for our current catalog describing these and many other books and gifts of interest to
investors and traders.

1-800-927-8222   FAX 864-298-0221
Tradersprs@aol.com

MARKET ART!

Market-related art available through
TRADERS PRESS.

If interested in full details, please contact:

TRADERS PRESS, INC.®
I N C O R P O R A T E D
P.O. BOX 6206
GREENVILLE, S.C. 29606

Books and Gifts
for Investors and Traders

1-800-927-8222   FAX 864-298-0221
Tradersprs@aol.com

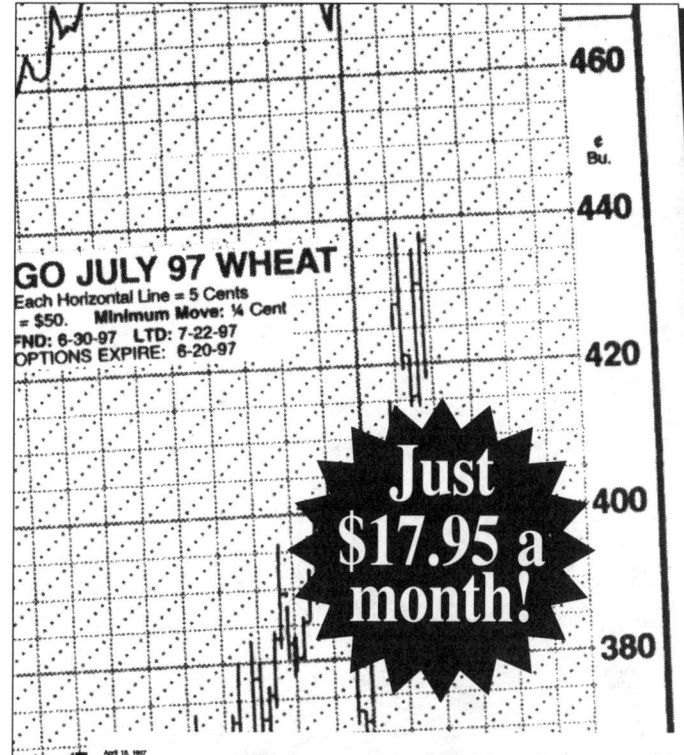

191

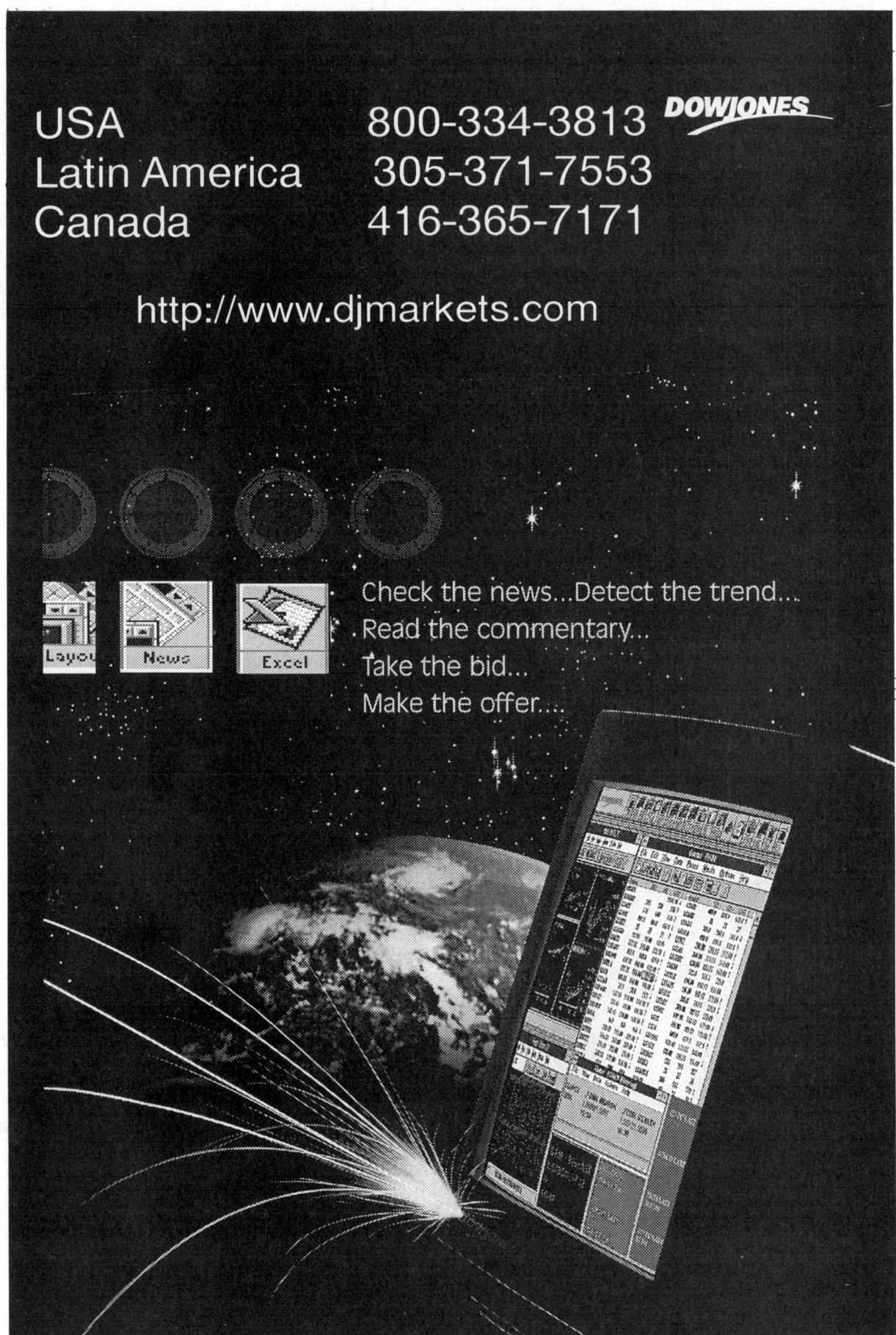